boys to MEN

Tim Gray received a master of theological studies degree in Scripture from Duke University and a master's degree in theology from Franciscan University of Steubenville. He is the author of *Mission of the Messiah,* a Bible study on the Gospel of Luke, and *Sacraments in Scripture.*

Curtis Martin is the founding president of the Fellowship of Catholic University Students (FOCUS), a dynamic college campus evangelization and leadership training program. He received his bachelor's degree in communications from Louisiana State University and his master's degree in theology from Franciscan University of Steubenville. He is the coauthor (with his wife, Michaelann) of *Family Matters: A Bible Study on Marriage and Family.*

boys to MEN

THE *TRANSFORMING* POWER OF VIRTUE

EMMAUS
ROAD
PUBLISHING

Steubenville, Ohio

Tim Gray and Curtis Martin

Emmaus Road Publishing
827 North Fourth Street
Steubenville, Ohio 43952

Library of Congress Control Number: 20-01086598
ISBN 1-931018-02-2

Cover design and layout
Beth Hart

Nihil Obstat: Rev. Philip Larrey, Ph.D., *Censor Deputatus*
December 15, 2000

Imprimatur: ✠ Charles J. Chaput, O.F.M. Cap., D.D., Archbishop of Denver
January 24, 2001

To Charles Coble,
a man of God and virtuous friend.

Contents

Acknowledgments

One of the subvirtues of justice is gratitude, and I would be very remiss if I did not thank my wife, Kris. Not only did she support and help me in a thousand ways so that this book could be written during a frantically busy summer, she devoted a considerable amount of time and talent to editing the chapters of this book as they were written. She is truly the best editor of what I write and what I do, both regarding this book and the book of life. Without her I would be without many of the virtues. Also, special thanks are due to Jayd Henricks. He toiled over the many drafts of this book and gave penetrating and enlightening advice. This book is surely better thanks to his keen suggestions and editing. Also, many thanks are due my good friend Curtis Martin. Writing a book on the virtues together with a friend is more than fitting, since friendship is one of the best fruits of the virtues. Aristotle believed that the goal of the virtues is to make us capable of being good friends. What could be better?

TIM GRAY

More than anything, I want to give thanks to God for the gift of my wife, Michaelann, who has been an example of virtue to me for more than a decade. Not only am I blessed by her consistent acts of love, I am especially amazed at her sense of joy in the midst of service. I also want to thank my children, Brock, Thomas, Augustine, MariAnna, Philip, and Joshua. As each of you struggle to grow and develop, you remind me of how Our Heavenly Father must look upon us. I love you, even in the midst of your failures. I only want you to rise again. Imagine how much more God must be willing to forgive us and love us, so that we too may rise again and conquer.

CURTIS MARTIN

Abbreviations

Old Testament
Gen./Genesis
Ex./Exodus
Lev./Leviticus
Num./Numbers
Deut./Deuteronomy
Josh./Joshua
Judg./Judges
Ruth/Ruth
1 Sam./1 Samuel
2 Sam./2 Samuel
1 Kings/1 Kings
2 Kings/2 Kings
1 Chron./1 Chronicles
2 Chron./2 Chronicles
Ezra/Ezra
Neh./Nehemiah
Tob./Tobit
Jud./Judith
Esther/Esther
Job/Job
Ps./Psalms
Prov./Proverbs
Eccles./Ecclesiastes
Song/Song of Solomon
Wis./Wisdom
Sir./Sirach (Ecclesiasticus)
Is./Isaiah
Jer./Jeremiah

Lam./Lamentations
Bar./Baruch
Ezek./Ezekiel
Dan./Daniel
Hos./Hosea
Joel/Joel
Amos/Amos
Obad./Obadiah
Jon./Jonah
Mic./Micah
Nahum/Nahum
Hab./Habakkuk
Zeph./Zephaniah
Hag./Haggai
Zech./Zechariah
Mal./Malachi
1 Mac./1 Maccabees
2 Mac./2 Maccabees

New Testament
Mt./Matthew
Mk./Mark
Lk./Luke
Jn./John
Acts/Acts of the Apostles
Rom./Romans
1 Cor./1 Corinthians
2 Cor./2 Corinthians
Gal./Galatians

Eph./Ephesians
Phil./Philippians
Col./Colossians
1 Thess./1 Thessalonians
2 Thess./2 Thessalonians
1 Tim./1 Timothy
2 Tim./2 Timothy
Tit./Titus
Philem./Philemon
Heb./Hebrews
Jas./James
1 Pet./1 Peter
2 Pet./2 Peter
1 Jn./1 John
2 Jn./2 John
3 Jn./3 John
Jude/Jude
Rev./Revelation (Apocalypse)

Chapter 1
Men and Virtue

Why Virtue?

Today it is more common to hear about values than virtues. Current thought is that society would be safe, healthy, and happy, if only we could instill proper values into people. Values-based moral education programs exemplify the modern conviction that morality is nothing other than the art of making good choices, which are guided entirely by one's own values. One could critique this approach to morality on philosophical grounds, but my criticism is simple and to the point. The problem is that values fall short when it comes to making men moral. Having good values is a fine thing, but the battle of morality is not so much about *knowing* what is right as it is *doing* what is right. The difference between wanting to do the good and actually doing it is tremendous. Thus, many men who commit adultery know what they are doing is wrong (no need for value clarification), but they are unfaithful despite their values. Right values do not always translate into right action.

Many men want to be good husbands and fathers, but if this wanting is not supplemented by the virtues—the skills for successful moral living—then success will be unlikely. For example, I can value flying, spend countless hours as a passenger, and be the most avid aviation fan around, but that does not enable me to fly a plane. In order to fly, one must have the skills of a pilot. Many people desire to fly a plane, but few have the ability. Similarly, if our moral life is to get off the ground, we must acquire the skills necessary to fly. Values alone will not suffice.

The Heart of the Problem

The reason that knowledge alone is not enough for success in the moral life stems from the fact that we have inherited a wounded nature. Since the fall of Adam and Eve, human nature is fallen from its original perfection. Saint Paul describes just how wounded our nature is:

> We know that the law is spiritual; but I am carnal, sold under sin. I do not understand my own actions. For I do not do what I want, but I do the very thing I hate. . . . I can will what is right, but I cannot do it. For I do not do the good I want, but the evil I do not want is what I do. . . . Wretched man that I am! Who will deliver me from this body of death? (Rom. 7:14-15, 18-19, 24).

This condition is an effect of original sin (cf. Catechism, no. 1707). Through original sin every individual is born with a human nature that is weak and inclined to commit personal sin (the theological term for this condition is *concupiscence*). The mind struggles with ignorance, the body suffers pain and death, and the passions tend to undermine our ability to know and do the good (cf. Catechism, no. 405). We fall into sin not so much out of ignorance but weakness. It is within this context that we understand the virtues as liberating powers, raising man above his fallen nature to the truth and beauty in which each person becomes the person he was created to be.

The weakness caused by original sin causes us to be inclined toward sin. The power of virtue is that it reverses the inclination toward evil, and by strength of habit inclines us toward the good. For example, we are inclined to lie when the truth will hurt us, but the man who has the virtue of honesty possesses the inclination to tell the truth. Virtues tip the scales of the moral life toward good and away from evil.

How can we do good and live a virtuous life given Saint Paul's account of our fallen nature? Are we bound to sin? No. Saint Paul gives an answer to the anguished cry, "Who will deliver me from this body of death?" when he goes on to give thanks to "God through Jesus Christ our Lord!" (Rom. 7:25). Paul then explains in Romans 8 how Christ has set us free from the captivity of sin and death. Through the power of the Holy Spirit, our fallen nature is healed, perfected, and elevated.

Thus Saint Paul says that through Baptism we have put on "the new nature" (cf. Col. 3:9-10). The grace and power of Jesus Christ transforms our old nature, referred to by Saint Paul in Romans 7. This means that we can live a virtuous life, thanks to Christ. It is important to note the careful balance between God's grace and our effort. Apart from God we can do nothing, and apart from our effort God cannot work in our lives. Both God's grace and our effort are needed.

Consider the analogy of a sailboat. The finest sailboat in the world can't sail far without its sails. Even with much wind and good weather, if the sails are not up, the boat will not make much headway. The sails signify our effort, namely the virtues. Conversely, if the boat has excellent sails but no wind, it cannot sail. The wind is like God's grace. We can make all the effort and preparation in the world, but without God's grace we will not make much progress in the moral life. Similarly, we can receive the sacraments and pray, but God's grace will not avail much if we do not act. The wind will pass over the ship without much effect because the sails are not up.

This happens to too many Christians. They go to Church and receive the sacraments, but the wind of God's grace passes by them, as they do not put much effort into following Christ. God may be present in our lives but, unless we cooperate with His action, we will not reach our destination of eternal life. Success in sailing through the troubled waters of the moral life requires us to rely on God and expend much effort at the same time. Loving God with all our strength will raise the sails so that they can catch God's grace, which will empower us to move across the rough waters of this world to the tranquil harbor of heaven. This is what the virtues are all about, our cooperation with God and His plan for our lives. Through the virtues, both human and theological, we enable God to fill the sails of our ship and move it in the right direction.

The virtuous life is critical because it is the path by which we reach the final purpose of life, eternal happiness. Every person is created for happiness, but final and complete happiness comes only after a life directed to the good that lies beyond our immediate needs or wants. Virtue should not be considered burdensome, but rather as liberating and as the path to personal happiness. Indeed, the ancient Greek philosopher Aristotle argued that substantial happiness and human flourishing could only be grasped through the virtues.

Virtues as Skills

To be a morally good person takes more than wishing to be good or having the right values. Rather, it takes a rock-solid character that has the strength to *will* what is right, not just *value* what is good. The will is that spiritual power of the soul by which we choose to do something. The strength to will the right thing is what is meant by the term virtue. "A virtue is an habitual and firm disposition to do the good" (Catechism, no. 1803). A virtue is a *good, habitual action of the will,* and not only is a virtue an action that is habitual, it is an action that is done with *promptness* and, in a certain sense, *pleasure.* For example, to truly have the virtue of honesty, it is not enough to tell the truth repeatedly, but to tell the truth repeatedly with ease and promptitude.

From another perspective, a virtue can be understood as the balance between opposing extremes. For example, courage is the virtue between cowardliness and rashness. Cowardice is to let fear overrun one's reason, while rashness is to be dull to all fear and act foolishly. In contrast, courage moderates fear and keeps it under the control of reason, avoiding the two extremes of caving into fear or being so numb to it as to act imprudently. The vices of cowardice and rashness lack the balance of the virtue of courage. As we examine the virtues, we shall briefly look at their opposing vices. It is important to realize that, just as the good habits we call virtues give us freedom and strength to do good, the bad habits we call vices take our freedom from us and incline us toward evil.

Virtues, as has already been stated, strengthen the will and dispose it to right action. Think of your will as a muscle. Just as an athlete strengthens and trains his muscles, be it a basketball player practicing a 3-point shot or a golfer working on his swing, we too must develop, strengthen, and train our wills to live virtuously. Just as Michael Jordan has developed the habit of making basketball shots, the virtuous person habitually, and with similar ease, does what is good. In the moral life, it is by practicing a virtue that we train and strengthen our wills and ultimately acquire the virtue. Similarly, just as muscles that are not exercised become flabby and weak, so too do our wills become weak if we are not exercising them by the practice of virtue.

Virtues are the necessary skills required to navigate our life through this world. They are the qualities that enable us to make life's journey successful. If I wanted to sail across the sea, it would take more than just desire. I cannot wish myself across the stormy seas, no matter how much I value sailing, ships, or safety. If I attempt the high seas without seamanship, all the values and desire in the world will be utterly worthless. Likewise, one can desire to be a good man, even a holy man, but without the virtues his moral life will be shipwrecked.

The Parable of the Twenty-Dollar Bill

The inner nature and workings of virtue can be hard to understand, so let's look at this story as an example.

Two men, each at different times, notice a twenty-dollar bill that is unattended at a co-worker's desk. The first man recognizes that he is alone in the office and that he could easily pocket the money without anyone's notice. He is strongly tempted to pocket the twenty-dollar bill. After great agony and hesitation, the man decides not to take the twenty. Later, another man comes through the office and sees the twenty-dollar bill, but he does not even consider stealing it and goes on to finish his errand at the copy room. Which man is virtuous?

Despite the fact that neither one sinned, only one exhibited virtue. The fact that it took the first man time and effort not to take the money illustrates that, despite his just act, he lacks the virtue of justice. One might ask how we can say the first man fails to have the virtue of justice when he did what was just? Because, as we discussed above, a virtue is more than one act, it is more than repeated action, it is a *disposition* to do the good with ease, promptitude, and joy. The first man's struggle illustrates his lack of virtue. He lacks the habitual disposition to give others their just due with ease. A virtue is more than doing the right thing, it is the power to do the right thing with the right attitude, with ease and joy. Thus the second man's act done with ease and lack of struggle displays the inherent power of virtue.

Despite the fact that our nature starts out weakened and inclined to sin because of concupiscence, it can be transformed by God's grace and the virtues (cf. Catechism, nos. 1264, 1266). The two men in the parable above illustrate this contrast. The first was inclined to take the money, but the virtuous man is inclined in the direction of doing the good. The inclination to do the good, which is a hallmark of virtue, demonstrates how the virtues give our nature a new bent. That is, the virtues transform our weakened nature and give it a new strength and the habitual disposition to will what is right.

A Bold New Blueprint

The acquisition of virtues is not easy. To be virtuous is an achievement. One cannot become a sailor in a day. Anything that requires skill, be it piloting a plane, playing a piano, or becoming a professional athlete, takes arduous effort. So too does the moral life. One cannot be a man of God, that is, truly virtuous, without constant effort and the grace of God.

The virtues give us a blueprint for being a man. Indeed, the very term *virtue* comes from the Latin word for man, *vir*. For the ancients, to be manly was to be virtuous. The term "virtue" in Latin (*virtus*) signifies power, strength, and ability. Thus the virtues are habits that give us the power to act in a manly way, with strength sufficient to do what is right. Without virtues we will neither be godly nor manly.

Men are made through the iron furnace of virtue. This profound insight is true, even if few recognize it. What makes a man is not how much money he makes or what kind of car he drives, but the character that he has forged through the practice of virtue. There is profound insight in the saying, "Sow a thought, reap an action; sow an action, reap a habit; sow a habit, reap a character; sow a character, reap a destiny." Virtues are the building blocks of character, and without them our moral lives will eventually collapse under the pressures of the world and we will fall short of our proper destiny.

Just Do It

Virtues are essential to living well and, even more, to living the Christian life well. Saint Peter exhorted the early Christians about the vital role of the virtues saying, "[M]ake every effort to supplement your faith with virtue" (2 Pet. 1:5). A few verses later, he admonishes us that practicing the virtues will keep us from being "ineffective or unfruitful" in following Jesus Christ (2 Pet. 1:8). In other words, our lives will only be as effective, meaningful, and fruitful as we are virtuous. No wonder Saint Peter admonishes us to "make every effort" to obtain virtue.

The saints and many biblical characters are strong witnesses of the virtuous life. As we examine each of the virtues, we will give an example of how that virtue is embodied by one of the saints. Sacred Scripture and the lives of the saints offer us many examples of the nobility and goodness of the virtuous life. The saints provide us with heroic models to imitate. Thus Saint Paul writes, "Brethren, join in imitating me, and mark those who so live as you have an example in us" (Phil. 3:17). More is caught than taught, and by reading the lives of the saints we may catch the inspiration and desire to live the wonderful life of virtue.

In the following chapters, we shall first look at the four cardinal virtues, followed by the three theological virtues, explaining them and considering how to grow in them. Justice, courage, temperance, and prudence are those natural virtues which are fundamental and essential for all the other human virtues. They are called *cardinal* virtues, from the Latin word *cardo*, which means "hinge," because the entire moral life hinges upon these four virtues. In short, they are the cornerstone for the moral life (cf. Catechism, no. 1805). The theological virtues of faith, hope, and love are those supernatural powers infused into the soul enabling the soul to participate in God's very life (cf. Catechism, no. 1813). We shall see how the virtues are skills that will empower us to navigate life's journey successfully.

We must make a firm resolution to grow in virtue. Saint Thomas Aquinas, one of the most brilliant men who ever lived, was once asked the secret to being a saint. He immediately replied with a two-word answer that has now become a marketing proverb: "Will it." And it is the virtues, along with God's grace, that empower us to do what we know is right, to *just do it.*

Questions

1. a. What is the practical difference between virtues and values?

_____

_____

b. Why are values alone insufficient for morality?

_____

_____

2. Read Romans 7:14-24. In this passage, Saint Paul says we are enslaved to sin. Do you agree with him? Do you find it easy to avoid sin, or do you find yourself doing the very thing you do not want to do? Rate yourself on the scale below.

$$1 \quad 2 \quad 3 \quad 4 \quad 5 \quad 6 \quad 7 \quad 8 \quad 9 \quad 10$$
Trapped in sin ——————————— _Easy to avoid sin_

3. In the very next verses (Rom. 7:25, 8:2), God gives us the only solution to our sin problem. The heart of the problem is our own broken hearts. Read Ezekiel 36:24-28. How will God's response go right to the "heart" of the problem?

_____

_____

4. Read 1 Corinthians 10:1-13. Why is a Bible study a good way to develop a vision for the virtues?

_____

_____

_____

_____

5. Saint Paul compares our lives to an athletic competition. Read 1 Corinthians 9:24-27 and 2 Timothy 4:7-8. How is life like a competition?

_____

_____

_____

_____

6. How is it different?

_____

_____

7. List the three qualities a good action must have in order to be truly virtuous (see p. 14).

a. _____

b. _____

c. _____

8. In Galatians 6:7-10, how does Saint Paul warn us that our actions will have consequences?

_____

_____

9. Read Genesis 27-29. Note how or what Jacob reaps from his earlier actions. How does Jacob's deception of his father, who was physically blind, come back to Jacob when he is unable to see? How is Jacob's marriage affected by his usurpation of his brother's birthright?

_____

_____

_____

_____

10. Are you ready to become the man God has made you to be? If not, what do you think is holding you back?

_____

_____

_____

_____

11. How can you begin to make better choices in your life?

_____

_____

12. Are there specific ways in which you have reaped what you have sown?

_____

_____

_____

_____

Memory Verse
"All Scripture is inspired by God and
profitable for teaching, for reproof, for correction,
and for training in righteousness,
that the man of God may be complete,
equipped for every good work."
2 Timothy 3:16-17

Chapter 2

Men of Prudence

What Is Wisdom?

We begin with the virtue of prudence because it is, as we shall see, the virtue that directs all the other virtues. In modern culture the word "prudence" often unfairly connotes negative images, such as a "prude" or a coward. This, however, is not an accurate portrayal of prudence. True prudence can lead one to dive on a grenade, fight courageously in battle, begin a huge investment venture, or be open to having a tenth child. Prudence does not mean timidity or undue cautiousness, but rather right judgment.

Prudence is almost synonymous with wisdom. Herein lies part of the problem, for many see wisdom as abstract knowledge, and they wonder how it can be a virtue. More importantly, how can anyone who is not a contemplative monk obtain it? Isn't wisdom accessible only after years of quiet reflection? The truth is, gray hair and a ragged white beard are not prerequisites for wisdom. David in his youth says, "I understand more than the aged, for I keep thy precepts" (Ps. 119:100). Wisdom is not up in the sky that you need to ask someone to bring it down to you; it is within everyone's reach.

According to Proverbs, Wisdom cries out to all in the streets and marketplaces, saying, "How long, O simple ones, will you love being simple? How long will scoffers delight in their scoffing and fools hate knowledge?" (Prov. 1:22). Wisdom is not just for the elite. It calls out to everyone, and not simply to priests, elders, and scribes. It is not for the elite alone. Indeed, the places where Wisdom cries out most noticeably are the marketplace and streets, the everyday places where normal life happens, not in the Temple or libraries. This is because God desires everyone to have a wisdom-formed prudence. Not only that, wisdom has a practical purpose which is to be used in the marketplace just as much, if not more, than in classrooms or libraries. Real wisdom (prudence) is not bookish learning; it is a practical and useful virtue for everyday life.

To many, prudence seems like a virtue necessary only for the important decisions of life, and not for daily living. What does prudence have to do with decisions like how bills should be paid, whether the family car should be kept for another year, whether it is time to find a new job, how to make the best investment decisions, where to send the kids to school, how late to set curfew, or what movie to rent for the family tonight? In other words, what does prudence have to do with everyday life? Far from being esoteric and abstract, prudence is exceedingly practical. Prudence is about navigating through life. Read the Book of Proverbs and you will find that it guides one to prudence through discussions about work, family life, friendship, and getting along with one's neighbors. Nothing could be more down-to-earth than good ol' prudence.

"*Prudence* is the virtue that disposes practical reason to discern our true good in every circumstance and to choose the right means of achieving it" (Catechism, no. 1806, original emphasis). Prudence guides one to do the right thing, at the right time, and in the right way. Prudence is the art of taking moral principles and applying them to concrete situations. For example, we know we should not get drunk, but prudence tells us here and now that this beer should be our last one. Prudence is, according to Saint Thomas Aquinas, right reason applied to action.[1] Saint Thomas breaks up prudence into three key steps: counsel, judgment, and decisiveness.

Judging what is the right thing to do, at the right time, and in the right way can sometimes be difficult. The first step is to take

---

[1] Saint Thomas Aquinas, *Summa Theologiae*, IIa IIae, q. 47, art. 2. Cited hereafter as *Summa*.

counsel from those who are prudent, experienced, and knowledgeable regarding the matter at hand (cf. Tob. 4:18). Thus, when buying a used car, the first step toward a prudent decision would be to seek counsel from a mechanic and/or someone who would know the car's market value. *Counsel* involves gathering all the information and advice that is necessary for making a right decision. The Book of Proverbs exhorts us to be sure to take counsel: "Without counsel plans go wrong, but with many advisers they succeed" (Prov. 15:22).

Judgment is the second step. After gathering information and advice, the evidence must be weighed. *Judgment* is the ability to apply all relevant principles and facts to the decision at hand. The Book of Sirach states that "a man of judgment will not overlook an idea" and then it goes on to say, "Do nothing without deliberation" (Sir. 32:18-19). The advice about the car, including its mileage, age, and asking price, are now weighed. "Is this a wise purchase?" Judgment answers the question about what is the right course of action.

Finally, once one judges what is the right thing to do, one must act. To take counsel and then judge what should be done, but to fail to do it, is to come up short on prudence. For Saint Thomas Aquinas, one must not only know what the right path is through prudence, but one must be *decisive* in acting on that knowledge. "Sometimes after judging aright we delay to execute or execute negligently or inordinately."[2] This failure of nerve means that one is not prudent, for prudence is also decisive.

The Key to Prudence

There is a simple principle to prudence, and once you understand that principle and learn to habitually apply it, you will become a man of wisdom. What is the secret of wisdom, this principle that gives one prudence? Saint Thomas Aquinas, known as

---

[2] *Summa*, IIa IIae, q. 51, art. 3.

the Angelic Doctor because of his great wisdom, describes the wise man as one who orders everything according to its end.[3]

This statement embodies a profound philosophy, but it is simpler than it sounds. According to Saint Thomas, the prudent man judges everything in view of its end (its final purpose), and then he ultimately makes the right decisions because he has the final goal in mind.

> The prudent man considers things afar off, in so far as they tend to be a help or a hindrance to that which has to be done at the present time. Hence it is clear that those things which prudence considers stand in relation to this other, as in relation to the end.[4]

Prudence is the virtue that chooses the way to reach a destination. As Proverbs says, "The wisdom of a prudent man is to discern his way" (Prov. 14:8).

Here's a simple example. Whenever you plan a family vacation, you decide first where you are going to go. Whether it will be Mount Rushmore in the Black Hills of South Dakota or the beaches of Florida, you begin with the end in mind. Once you have chosen your destination, you plan how you are going to get there. Will you travel by car or take a plane? You measure the costs the trip will incur. You determine the likely weather and you pack accordingly. But notice that how you pack and prepare depends on where you are going. All the decisions about the family vacation usually revolve around where your destination lies or, to use the philosophical term, what your end is.

Prudence is the ability to discern the best means to achieving the right goals or ends. But it cannot be overemphasized how important it is to know what the objective is, for without the goal in mind one will never reach the right destination. Aim for nothing, and you will hit it every time. Having the goal in mind

---

[3] *Summa*, IIa IIae, q. 47, art. 7.
[4] *Summa*, IIa IIae, q. 47, art. 1.

is of immense practical benefit. The story of Coach Homer Rice exemplifies the practical importance of having goals. Rice compiled a spectacular record as a high school football coach in Kentucky. When Rice was a young coach, he would write down specific goals for the season and for each game. Each goal had a deadline, and Rice believed that the key to his success was the clear objectives that he daily reviewed. Deadlines are crucial, for a goal without a deadline is a dream.

After awhile Rice shared his method with his football players. Each of the players on his team set concrete goals for each game, such as cause two fumbles, rush for 100 yards, sack the quarterback twice, catch four passes. Rice's players rose to a remarkable level of achievement (for example, a 50-game undefeated streak, five straight championships, etc.). Coach Rice and his football players embodied prudence. They judged how to use their time and energy based on what their goals were. Prudence can be practical and, as Coach Rice's football players realized, prudence can make the difference between winning and losing.

This principle of judging things in light of their final end is the master key of wisdom. "The prudent [man] looks where he is going" (Prov. 14:15). If you want to be an Olympic athlete, you make decisions daily about what you can eat or drink and, because of your goal, you may decide that certain foods, drinks, and drugs are not good to take. Such decisions are made in light of the goal. The leading question of discernment is, "Will this advance me or detract me from my purpose or goal?" The wise man puts all his decisions through this litmus test. How will buying a new stereo fit my plans to save up for a house? Will the golf outing on Saturday be a good use of time given my family's needs? Wisdom is crucial in how we spend the two key commodities given to us by God, our time and our money (gained from our talents). How to use our time and money wisely is crucial for becoming successful not only in the business world, but in the most important world of all, that of family and faith.

The North Star of Wisdom

Prudence directs the other cardinal virtues: justice, temperance, and courage. Indeed, the ancients called prudence the *auriga virtutum*, the charioteer of the virtues (Catechism, no. 1806). Prudence guides the way and the other virtues are put into action. For example, prudence might judge that having another beer would lead one to intoxication. Following the lead of this prudential judgment, the virtue of temperance then comes into play, giving one the strength to have a glass of water rather than another Guinness. Without prudence, the virtues of justice, fortitude, and temperance are not attainable. Virtues without prudence will run off the track like a chariot without a driver.

Prudence is in the driver's seat when it comes to the practice of virtue, and the key to good driving is knowing your ultimate destination. For the Christian, this destination is eternal life. Our purpose in life is to attain eternal life, both for ourselves and to help those around us reach it as well. Saint Augustine notes this well: "Prudence is love discerning aright that which helps from that which hinders us in tending to God."[5] With this end in mind, the prudent man orders his life to this final end. Everything is judged as to whether or not it helps him in this goal. This is the secret of life—knowing the purpose of life and making choices accordingly. "Prudence disposes the practical reason to discern, in every circumstance, our true good and to choose the right means for achieving it" (Catechism, no. 1835). We are not all called to live as contemplative monks, but we are called to have a supernatural motivation behind our activities, whether they are faith, family, business, or recreation. Ordering our whole lives to the goal of salvation sanctifies everything we do.

---

[5] Saint Augustine, *De Moribus Ecclesiae Catholicae et de Moribus Manichaeorum*, 22, as quoted in *Summa*, IIa IIae, q. 47, art. 1.

Men as Charioteers

Scripture exhorts men to lead their families. The Christian understanding of the father's headship at home is not that he is to be served as a tyrant, but that he is to serve his family by providing fatherly guidance and love. We cannot take on this whole topic here, but let's just focus briefly on how the father is to guide his family wisely by how he spends his time and money. How many men run successful businesses but utterly fail to lead their families? A good businessman knows he needs a budget and that he must manage his money carefully. Too often, however, men do not manage their family budget and finances well. Indeed, too many do not even have a family budget or financial plan. The net result is that money is simply spent at random, and thus family resources are wasted on things that are secondary. For example, money that could be used to pay off the car or house is wasted on a boat or other nonessential things, and the family gets into debt. Money problems are frequently a contributing factor to divorce. Not dealing wisely with money can damage not only the goals of the family, such as paying for college or private schooling, family vacations, a larger house, or tithing, but imprudent spending leads to tension with one's spouse. These problems would be minimized by practicing prudence in deciding what is most important (in light of the family's end and financial goals) and making a budget. Sticking to the budget is a matter of posing the key question of prudence: Does this put us closer or further from our goals (end)?

Spending our time also demands wisdom. Too often today we get so busy at work that we neglect our families. It is often said that when a man dies, he will not regret not spending enough time at the office, but rather not spending enough time at home. The principle of prudence is judging things by their end. A corollary principle is putting first things first. If we say that the most important part of our lives is our wives and children, then why do we spend so much of our precious free time putting in overtime at work or focusing on our own hobbies, such as cars or golf, and not with our families? Not that work or hobbies are bad, they just need to be properly ordered. We can neglect giving time to those we love without even realizing it. For example, after coming home from work (usually late), what is the first thing we do when we open the door and come in? Do we look for our spouses and children first, or do we go straight to the refrigerator or TV? How high on our list of priorities are sports? Do we spend more time watching football than playing with our kids or talking with our wives? Prudence is the virtue that allows us to put our true priorities into action (Catechism, no. 1780).

Growth in Prudence

Prudence can certainly be gained through time, but experience is not the only source for prudence. The Book of Proverbs begins by stating that wisdom is being written down so the simple and young may gain wisdom (cf. Prov. 1:2-5). Proverbs is punctuated by the exhortation of a father to his son: "Hear, my son, your father's instruction, and reject not your mother's teaching" (Prov. 1:8). Wisdom can be gained by experience, but it can also be passed on to the young through tradition. Learning from the father's experiences gives a youth wisdom beyond his years. Indeed, this is the primary purpose of tradition, to pass on wisdom to the next generation. This is demonstrated in crafts, where the master mentors the apprentice. And through successive generations, the craftsmen pass on an ongoing and deeper wisdom. Think of aviation, for example. The Wright brothers learned much about flying through trial and error, and the experience and wisdom gained by the Wright brothers has been passed on and deepened by generations of engineers and aviation professionals.

Learning from others is one of the primary ways we can grow in wisdom and prudence. This can happen in a variety of ways. First, one can learn from the lives and stories of many in the past. Salvation history teaches us much wisdom as we learn from

Abraham, Jacob, Saul, and Solomon how to better follow the Lord, learning from their successes and their failures. Thus, Scripture is a great resource for wisdom, for as we read the lives of the people of God we acquire wisdom from their life experiences.

One of the best ways to learn from others is to find a mentor, someone who is more experienced in life and in following Christ (cf. Catechism, no. 1788). This person, like an older brother, can provide counsel and perspective that can help us discern wisdom for following Christ and leading a virtuous life. This takes a certain *docility*, that is, we must have a teachable spirit. If we do not have the humility to ask and learn from others, we will miss one of the easiest and best paths to wisdom. One of the great challenges in this area, but one of tremendous value, is being able to accept correction. We all make mistakes, but to be man enough to take ownership and responsibility for them, and to have the courage to see them when they are pointed out, is the key to real growth in virtue. This truth is emphasized in Israel's wisdom literature: "My son, do not despise the LORD's discipline or be weary of his reproof, for the LORD reproves him whom he loves, as a father the son in whom he delights" (Prov. 3:11-12).

Questions

1. When all is said and done, what do you want your life to have stood for?

_____

_____

_____

2. a. What do you want to leave behind for your grandchildren and great-grandchildren?

_____

_____

b. What are you currently doing to make that happen?

_____

_____

c. How can you better order your priorities to reflect your goals?

_____

_____

_____

3. How does the adage "aim for nothing and you will hit it every time" apply to times in your life where you failed to achieve something?

_____

_____

4. According to the following passages, how do we acquire the virtue of prudence/wisdom?

a. Proverbs 2:3-5

_____

_____

b. Sirach 1:9-10

_____

_____

c. Matthew 7:7-8

_____

_____

d. James 1:5

_____

_____

5. What is the secret to David's wisdom, even as a young man, according to Psalm 119:97-104?

_____

_____

6. According to Saint Paul, why was the Old Testament given to us? (See 1 Corinthians 10:1-5, 11-13.)

_____

_____

7. Read Matthew 7:24-27. Both the wise man and the fool hear the Word of God. What is the difference between them?

_____

_____

8. What do the following passages tell us about wisdom?

a. Sirach 1:1

_____

_____

b. Proverbs 8:11

_____

_____

c. Proverbs 9:8-10

_____

_____

d. Proverbs 13:20

_____

_____

e. Proverbs 14:15

_____

_____

f. Proverbs 15:2

_____

_____

g. Proverbs 16:22

_____

_____

h. Matthew 10:16

_____

_____

9. Read Philippians 3:4-14. How does Saint Paul exemplify prudence?

_____

_____

10. Given our call to eternal life, what changes should you make to live more wisely?

_____

_____

11. Psalm 37:30 says that the righteous utter wisdom and their tongues speak justice. According to the next verse (v. 31), the footsteps of the wise do not slip. Why?

_____

_____

12. How might you imprint the Law of God on your heart and grow in wisdom?

_____

_____

_____

Memory Verse
"I have laid up thy word in my heart,
that I might not sin against thee."
Psalm 119:11

Chapter 3

**Men of Justice**

When we think of justice, images of a judge, jury, and court-room immediately come to mind. Justice is a judge handing down a solemn verdict. It is a criminal getting his punishment. This, however, is not the full meaning of justice. We need a broader vision of justice, one that goes beyond TV's view of the courtroom. Justice is the virtue that enables us to live rightly with others. Justice as a virtue empowers us to take care of others and give them what they deserve and need. Justice means right rela-tions not only with our neighbor, but most importantly with God Himself. "Justice consists in the firm and constant will to give God and neighbor their due" (Catechism, no. 1836).

Today we tend to view justice from the wrong perspective. Rather than considering what I owe others, the tendency is to ask, "What is owed me?" The burden of debt is on others rather than myself. In this sense, justice has become a principle of taking rather than giving. Even young children feel the effects of this selfish attitude. One of their first complaints in life is inevitably, "It's not fair!" Sin leads us to reject our responsibilities toward others and embrace a "me first" mentality. After Cain murdered his brother, God asked him, "Where is your brother Abel?" Cain responds, "Am I my brother's keeper?" (cf. Gen. 4:9). In contrast, we are told that Saint Joseph, the foster father of Christ, was a just man. When Joseph first learns of his bride's pregnancy (before he learns of the divine agency of Mary's pregnancy), he seeks not his own rights but a quiet resolution that would not hurt Mary (Mt. 1:19). Joseph invested his life in the care of Jesus and Mary. He was a man for others. He was a just man.

Justice is the virtue that inclines us to give others their due, giving them the respect and honor due to all persons who are made in the image and likeness of God. Courage and temperance are aimed at the interior man; they foster self-mastery. Justice, on the other hand, is aimed at the exterior—it orders our relations with others. The virtue of justice is the habit and disposition to give others what is rightly theirs. Charity goes further by giving to others what is rightfully our own. Even though charity surpasses justice, there can be no true charity without justice. Love must be built upon the firm foundation of justice.

In our daily activities we enter into countless situations that call for an application of justice: from purchasing something at the store, to work at the office, to respecting someone else's property (Catechism, no. 2401). Philosophers and social scientists distinguish among several forms of justice. For our purposes here, let's simplify the discussion by looking at justice from the perspective of work and family, since these are the areas where we daily practice justice. We will also examine how justice relates to God and to the allied virtue of truthfulness, and finally, how justice should be shaped by mercy.

God

The most important area of justice, known as the virtue of *religion*, is that which is owed to God. As creatures wholly dependent upon God for life, justice requires that we worship God as our Creator and final goal (Catechism, nos. 2095-96). The first three commandments explicitly oblige us to worship God. The First Commandment embodies this fundamental debt we as creatures owe to God: "You shall worship the Lord your God and him only shall you serve" (Mt. 4:10; cf. Deut. 5:6-9). By worship, we do not mean simply honor or respect. We may (or may not) respect the President, but we *worship* God. Worship is the reverence and adoration given to God alone as Creator and Savior (Catechism, no. 2703).

The Second Commandment speaks about the honor and reverence we are to give God's name. "You shall not take the name of the LORD your God in vain" (Deut. 5:11). This means we are not to violate the sacredness of God's name by cursing or by committing perjury.

The Third Commandment concerns the Sabbath. This commandment teaches us that the debt we owe God for creating and redeeming us must be given public acknowledgment by praising and thanking Him at Mass. Attending Mass on Sundays, therefore, is not simply the fulfillment of Church law, but a matter of justice. Indeed, Saint Paul observes that the beginning of one's falling away from God is the failure to give God the thanks and honor due to Him. This failure leads to a free fall into the worst kinds of sins and depravity, all of which begin with a failure to worship (cf. Rom. 1:21-27).

The rest of the Ten Commandments relate to justice owed to other human persons. As Saint John observed, to truly love God is to love our neighbor (cf. 1 Jn. 4:20). So now we shall examine some of the key areas in our lives where the virtue of justice must be lived out.

Work

Work is a basic component of human life. It should not be seen as a curse or necessary evil. From the beginning, God has called man to subdue the earth in wise stewardship. "Hence work is a duty: 'If any one will not work, let him not eat' (2 Thess. 3:10)" (Catechism, no. 2427). Work is a central part of man's vocation, and the virtue of justice enables him to fulfill his vocation to work, by which man honors his Creator and takes care of the needs of others.

Too often we view work as a necessary evil that impedes our fulfillment, but this is not true. It is vital to note that work was given to man *before* the Fall; it is not of itself a curse. The toil, sweat, and thorns that follow the Fall add an element of suffering to the vocation of work, but work itself is noble. Indeed, the suffering and hardship that often accompany work can be offered up by the Christian man so as to become a means of sanctification and conformity to the sacrifice of Christ Himself (cf. Col. 1:24).

> By enduring the hardship of work in union with Jesus, the carpenter of Nazareth and the one crucified on Calvary, man collaborates in a certain fashion with the Son of God in his redemptive work. He shows himself to be a disciple of Christ by carrying the cross, daily, in the work he is called to accomplish (Catechism, no. 2427).

Work, offered up to God and done to the best of one's abilities, is a sacrifice pleasing to God.

Another motive for work is the ability to share generously with the poor. Besides providing for one's family, work can provide means to support one's community, the Church, and the poor. "Love for the poor is even one of the motives for the duty of working so as to 'be able to give to those in need'" (Catechism, no. 2444, quoting Ephesians 4:28). Justice teaches us that all good things are a gift from our Father in heaven, and grateful stewardship will lead us to generosity with the poor. Love of the poor for the sake of Christ is a great way to sanctify one's work, for the fruits of one's labor offered to the needy is "a fragrant offering, a sacrifice acceptable and pleasing to God" (Phil. 4:18).

Our employer deserves our best effort. Poor work performance or simply "killing time" are injustices to our employer and offenses against our Creator and Lord. Saint Paul reminded the early Christians that whatever their work was and whoever it was for, they worked ultimately for God. Thus their job should be done with the utmost care and effort.

> Whatever your task, work heartily, as serving the Lord and not men, knowing that from the Lord you will receive the inheritance as your reward; you are serving the Lord Christ (Col. 3:23-24).

Work performed well and in honor of God will have an eternal compensation package according to Saint Paul.

No matter what our work is, whether it is governing the nation, flying a plane, making sales calls, or mowing the lawn, our work can be sanctified and offered to the glory of God. As Saint Thérèse of Lisieux observed, it is not the work we do, but the love we put into it that matters. Washing the dishes can be a means of holiness and love, if offered up to God with a cheerful heart. "Work can be a means of sanctification and a way of animating earthly realities with the Spirit of Christ" (Catechism, no. 2427).

Undoubtedly, the virtue of justice demands conscientiously fulfilling the requirements of a job, but it also implies a rightly ordered balance between what is due to our work and what is due to our family. First, this means that everyone has the right to a just wage, which means that a man should be able to draw from his work the means of providing for himself and his family. Second, it means that the family cannot be sacrificed for the sake of work and profit. Performing one's work well is virtuous, but becoming a workaholic is to turn the virtue into a vice. "Work is for man, not man for work" (Catechism, no. 2428).

Work and Family

Work is good, but if family, friends, and God are neglected as a result of our work, it can be a serious fault. One reason that men are prone to overwork is that men, in general, derive their self-esteem from their work. Men must make an effort to find a balance between working to support their families, without working so much that they tear down their families through neglect.

How is it that men can be so successful in the business world and such failures at home? It may well be that they take business seriously, having plans, goals, and training. But when it comes to being a husband and father, they have no job description or goals. Once again, aim for nothing and you will hit it every time. The key to success at home is for men to see that their work does not end when they come home, but rather that's when their work truly begins. While it may be difficult to replace a man in the workplace, it is impossible to replace him at home.

Another temptation that would lead us to put work above all else is greed. "For the love of money is the root of all evils; it is through this craving that some have wandered away from the faith and pierced their hearts with many pangs" (1 Tim. 6:10). Men must remember that giving good things to their children does not compare with giving themselves to their children. The wise father desires his children to have virtues and discipline more than money and possessions. Avarice or greed is considered one of the seven deadly sins because it consumes the sinner. We can't put all our time and energy into our work to the detriment of family and God: "For where your treasure is, there will your heart be also" (Mt. 6:21). We can always get more money, but we can never get back more time. Time is the great treasure we give to our families, because it is the gift of our very selves.

Even our family relationships are governed by justice. Relationships within a family are based on love for one another. Fathers, in particular, need to be concerned about giving to their families what is due them. Spending too much time at work and not being available for their children is against the order of justice. Children have the right to expect their fathers to be involved in their lives. Whether it is helping his son with his first steps, or his daughter with homework, or coaching a team sport, fathers ought to be present (cf. Catechism, no. 2223).

Spousal relationships also have a dimension of justice. Not being attentive to the needs of one's wife, whether material or emotional, is unjust. How many homes are destroyed because the husband is not available to his wife and children? Men must recover a sense of responsibility toward their families in ways that go beyond the financial stability of the household. It is, among other things, a matter of justice.

Community

The broader social community is another context for the application of justice. In the interest of the common good, society has the right to require services or payments (taxes) from individuals. The Scriptures speak about the legitimate authority of government as having been established by God (cf. Rom. 13). This authority is obviously not spiritual, but serves the basic physical needs of a society. To build roads, for example, a state can require the payment of a tax. Or, to protect the environment, government can forbid environmentally harmful activities. In anticipation of a just war, a draft may be held in order to secure peace and justice (cf. Catechism, nos. 2239-40, 2309). However, government may not place demands on individuals that go against divine or natural law, nor may it go beyond its limited authority with respect to policy or taxes. For example, justice does not allow for the freedom to take innocent life (cf. Catechism, no. 2273) or the usurpation of individual responsibility. Social justice always serves individual rights and the good of society (cf. Catechism, no. 1928).

Truthfulness

Truthfulness is needed in our relationship with God, family, friends, and everyone with whom we come into contact. "The eighth commandment forbids misrepresenting the truth in our relations with others" (Catechism, no. 2464). God is truth Himself, so those who follow Him must also be true in word and deed. It is Satan who is the "father of lies." Given the dignity of the human person, truth is owed to others out of justice; it is their due. Truthfulness implies sincerity, candor, and integrity. "Truth or truthfulness is the virtue which consists in showing oneself true in deeds and truthful in words, and in guarding against duplicity, dissimulation, and hypocrisy" (Catechism, no. 2468).

Truthfulness is a subvirtue of justice. The virtue of truth gives another their just due. Without truth society would not function.

Trust is essential to both good relations and a good economy. In a country where bribes and backhanded deals are made, the economy cannot function well. Truthfulness is key for human flourishing. Persons are due the truth, but that does not mean that we rudely or crudely tell people the truth. "Truthfulness keeps to the just mean between what ought to be expressed and what ought to be kept secret: it entails honesty and discretion" (Catechism, no. 2469). Our family and friends have a particular demand on our truthfulness.

Justice and Mercy

We must constantly remind ourselves that justice is first about what I owe others and not what is owed me. "Justice is the moral virtue that consists in the constant and firm will to give their due to God and neighbor" (Catechism, no. 1807). It is a *disposition* to look after the needs of others and to give God the glory as the source of all goodness. One is not just unless he is inclined to always give God and others what is rightly theirs. But, in addition to giving others what is properly theirs, we can always offer more. Through *mercy* and charity we go beyond the minimum require-ments of justice and give to others in excess.

From the Christian perspective, justice should be accompanied by mercy. Because it is easy to lose sight of what is a proper proportion (what is strictly just), it is proper to give more than what is simply just. As history has taught us, without attention to mercy, justice can easily become oppressive.

A biblical story that illustrates a mercy-shaped justice is David's relationship with Saul. After serving King Saul for some time, with heroic service and loyalty, David was unjustly charged by his king with treason. David fled for his life, and lived for some time in the wilderness, roaming and hiding as a hunted man. One day when Saul's army was closing in on David and his motley group of friends, Saul turned aside to a nearby cave to relieve himself. It just happened that David and his men were hiding in the same cave! David and his armed men found Saul in a very vulnerable position, to say the least. David's men encouraged him to kill Saul then and there. But David refused to strike down the man who had maligned David's name and was seeking his death: "The LORD forbid that I should do this thing to my lord, the LORD's anointed, to put forth my hand against him, seeing he is the LORD's anointed" (1 Sam. 24:6). David tempered his men with mercy. David respected Saul's holy office of king, even though Saul himself was wicked.

After Saul realized that David had refrained from killing him, he confessed that David was the one who was truly just. Saul declared:

> You are more righteous than I; for you have repaid me good, whereas I have repaid you evil. And you have declared this day how you have dealt well with me, in that you did not kill me when the LORD put me into your hands (1 Sam. 24:17-18).

David repaid evil with good, making his justice merciful.

The Scriptures tell us that the man who acts justly is called *righteous.* He is righteous because he has right relations with everyone. The virtue of justice turns our attention to others and to God, calling us to make things right in the world. This begins with offering worship and thanksgiving to God but overflows to care for others. Christians have a special duty to take care of others and influence the world around them because Christ commissioned us to be a light to the world.

The obligation of justice toward others is spoken of frequently throughout Scripture. How we care for other people is a critical element of our religious response to God. "Religion that is pure and undefiled before God and the Father is this: to visit orphans and widows in their affliction, and to keep oneself unstained from the world" (Jas. 1:27).

Our Lord teaches us that we will be judged according to our treatment of others:

> Then the king will say to those on His right hand, "Come, O blessed of my Father, inherit the kingdom prepared for you from the foundation of the world; for I was hungry and you gave me food, I was thirsty and you gave me drink, I was a stranger and you welcomed me, I was naked and you clothed me, I was sick and you visited me, I was in prison and you came to me" (Mt. 25:34-36).

It is true that whatever we do for our neighbor, especially the poor, we really do to Christ. But it is also true that a man who has been faithful to his wife and children will hear Jesus say to him, "You clothed me, you fed me, you gave me to drink, and you welcomed me by spending time with me and playing with me." By providing for his family's needs, a man will have not only loved his wife and children, but Jesus Christ as well.

When justice is transformed by supernatural grace, we recognize that what others need and what is required of us take on an eternal dimension. Our faith reinforces the need to care for the poor and honor those in authority, but it adds a new and challenging dimension. Because of the mercy we have been shown in Christ, who has freely forgiven us, we too are called to be men of mercy and forgiveness. Jesus taught us to remind ourselves of this when we pray, "Forgive us our trespasses as we forgive those who trespass against us."

Questions

Let's look at what the Scriptures teach concerning our responsibility to live the virtue of justice. How are we to act in justice with the following persons and situations?

God

1. Read Matthew 22:36-40. What does God expect from us?

_____

_____

2. Read Matthew 5:6. What does God promise us if we seek justice and righteousness?

_____

_____

Church

3. Read Romans 12:5-18. Because we are united in Christ, what is our relationship to one another?

_____

_____

4. How are we to treat one another?

_____

_____

5. Read Malachi 3:7-10.

a. What does Scripture say about our obligation to support the Church?

_____

_____

b. How does God view those who fail to support the Church?

_____

_____

6. According to Malachi and Philippians 4:17, why do we give to the Church? (See also Catechism, nos. 1351, 2043.)

_____

_____

Others

7. Read Matthew 18:21-35. According to Jesus, how will God's justice be applied in our lives?

_____

_____

8. Read Matthew 25:31-40. According to Jesus, how will we be judged?

_____

_____

Work

9. Read Colossians 3:23. If we were to live this precept, how would it affect our work?

_____

_____

10. Read Ephesians 6:5-8. If even a slave was to honor his master, how much more should we honor our employers?

_____

_____

Authority

11. Read John 19:10-11. Where does earthly authority come from?

_____

_____

12. Read 1 Samuel 24:1-17. How does David exemplify justice?

_____

_____

13. Read Romans 13:1-5. Nero was the Emperor of Rome when Saint Paul wrote this, and he eventually executed Paul. Do we give those in authority the honor they deserve?

_____

_____

Spouse

14. Read 1 Peter 3:7. What is the effect of not honoring your wife?

_____

_____

_____

15. Read Ephesians 5:25-32. What is our model and power for loving our wives?

_____

_____

_____

Children

16. Read Proverbs 22:6. What is our goal as fathers?

_____

_____

17. Read Ephesians 6:4. What do we need to give our children in order for them to succeed?

_____

_____

18. Read Colossians 3:21. How can we protect the hearts of our children?

_____

_____

19. After reading this chapter, what specific changes can you make in your daily life to be a more just man, spouse, father, and employee?

_____

_____

_____

_____

Memory Verse
"But God shows forth his love for us
in that while we were yet sinners
Christ died for us."
Romans 5:8

Chapter 4

Men of Fortitude

Of all the virtues, fortitude is the one that is most often associated with men. Men are supposed to be tough and strong, and therefore courageous. Too often, however, this association gives us a narrow picture of fortitude, a picture that sees courage as only good for fighting. Undoubtedly, soldiers need to be fortified with courage, but courage is bigger than the battlefield. Courage is required in a number of ways that we seldom realize. For example, did you know that to be generous with material items and money takes courage? The things that require the virtue of courage can range from taking care of someone with a serious illness, persevering in a difficult task, taking a plane trip, or simply studying. Indeed, the virtue of courage is so basic that we need it to practice the other virtues.

What Is Fortitude?

Fortitude is courage, and for our purposes we will use the two terms interchangeably. Courage is the strength of will that enables us to conquer fear.

> *Fortitude* is the moral virtue that ensures firmness in difficulties and constancy in the pursuit of the good. It strengthens the resolve to resist temptations and to overcome obstacles in the moral life (Catechism, no. 1808, original emphasis).

At times, courage is what allows us to overcome fear, and, at other times, courage restrains excessive boldness. Often fear keeps us from acting, but there are circumstances when the bravest and most difficult thing to do is wait patiently and endure. Thus, courage steers a middle course between cowardliness on one side and foolhardiness on the other. As Saint Thomas Aquinas says, "Therefore fortitude is about fear and daring, as curbing fear and moderating daring."[1]

The Weak of Heart

It often happens that we know what we ought to do, but we're afraid to do it because of the consequences we may suffer as a result. Fear makes our will hesitant to follow reason because of the perceived difficulty. Consequently, we allow fear to determine our actions, rather than acting according to what is right according to God's will and law. Courage empowers us to have the firmness of mind and will to overcome our fear and do what is right and good, regardless of any difficulty. Thus Saint Thomas Aquinas says, "Fortitude of soul must be that which binds the will firmly to the good of reason in face of the greatest evils."[2]

Fear can be so strong that it prevents people from acting. For example, some people may fear to fly, and thus their fear keeps them from traveling, whether for business, family, or faith. Imagine if Saint Paul had been overcome by fear of sailing (traveling by ship in his day was far more dangerous than by plane in our own) and decided not to evangelize much of the Roman Empire. Some people may fear a change in life. What if Beethoven had succumbed to his fears and stopped writing symphonies after he went deaf? Much good can be lost through fear.

Almost anything that entails difficulty requires the virtue of courage. Indeed, Aristotle claimed that an element of courage was needed for the practice of all the virtues. "A firm standing is necessary in every virtue."[3] This firmness of mind and will that

---

[1] *Summa*, IIa IIae, q. 123, art. 3.
[2] *Summa*, IIa IIae, q. 123, art. 4.
[3] *Nicomachean Ethics*, book II, chap. 1.

courage provides is required in countless daily activities. A student may fear to take the best course in his field because the professor is demanding. A politician may fail to vote according to his principles out of fear of losing votes. A man may refrain from evangelizing a coworker out of fear of how he will be regarded or out of fear of not being able to answer every objection. Some people are afraid to learn a new skill, like using a computer, because it seems too complicated for them. Most of us fear to say no to others because we want to be liked. How many fathers, for example, fail to discipline their children for fear that their children will not like them? People fail to be honest out of fear. Whenever we lie or "fudge" the truth, it is because we fear that telling the truth will cause us some kind of grief.

A good example of this is Peter's denial of Jesus. Immediately following the shocking betrayal and arrest of Jesus, Peter finds his way through to the court of the high priest, just outside of the place where Jesus was being tried. Standing by the charcoal fire to warm himself from the cold night, Peter is asked three times if he is a disciple of Jesus. Each time Peter denies that he knows Jesus (Jn. 18:15-27). Peter lies out of fear—fear that he too may be arrested. This fear causes Peter not simply to lie, but to deny his Lord and Savior, Jesus Christ. Here Peter fails to be both courageous and just, by lying to others and most of all by denying the love and devotion due to Jesus. Courage is needed to be faithful to oneself and others.

No Pain, No Gain

Fear creates cowards, men who give up the truth or some good for fear of suffering. It hinders us from being men of action: It is much safer to be a spectator in life. Courage, on the other hand, empowers us to take on what is hard and persevere through the difficulties. It fortifies a spirit of strength and self-control (cf. 2 Tim. 1:7). "Fortitude ensures firmness in difficulties and constancy in the pursuit of the good" (Catechism, no. 1837).

Nothing ventured, nothing gained. The key to being a successful man of action is to be a man of courage. This virtue gives us the resolve to resist temptations and to overcome obstacles in the moral life. Even in the business world, those who have the courage to prudently take risks, to begin the difficult projects, and persevere in the face of adversity are the ones who are the most successful. So too, in the moral life: Those who are willing to take prudent risks for the sake of Christ will grow in grace and virtue.

As compared to all other people, Christians have the greatest reason to take courage. Our God is the God of all creation and has redeemed us and freed us from the powers of evil. In Joshua 1:5-9, what does God repeatedly say to Joshua before his mission? What reason does God give for Joshua's courage? God says to him and to all of us, "Have I not commanded you? Be strong and of good courage; be not frightened, neither be dismayed; for the LORD your God is with you wherever you go" (Josh. 1:9).

God Himself is with us. In fact, as a result of our Baptism, God dwells in us. We have access to His grace and, as a result, we have reason to take courage in all situations, regardless of the difficulties that we may encounter (cf. Heb. 13:6). God does not want us to be fearful, but to trust in His providential love for us.

Knowledge of God's love for us is a major motive to be courageous. If we did not know that the God who made us loves us so much that He desires to remake us in the image of His Son Jesus, then we would fail to have the courage to be Christian. The Christian man has the courage to call God "Father" because of his hope in God's mercy. Without God's merciful love we could not face our sins—the knowledge of them would destroy us.

The Christian story of Christ's merciful love for sinners teaches us to trust in God. This allows us to have the courage to acknowledge and confess our sins. Confession takes courage. When we go to the priest in the Sacrament of Confession, we are exhibiting courage, a courage based on the merciful love of

God. Too often men fail to face their sins and faults out of fear—fear of who they are and what they have done. But this need not be, as Jesus Christ has come to free us from the bondage of our shame and sin, and remake us through His grace and the life of virtue.

Courage can make us man enough to admit our faults, to take ownership of our shortcomings and sins. This virtue enables us to be humble and forthright enough to go to the confessional and tell God what we have failed to do, and make a firm resolution to set things right with His help. The danger is to be too afraid to face our sins, to want to hide from the truth just as Adam hid from God in the garden. Cowardliness, not manly courage, would lead us to say to Jesus, "Get away from me, for I am a sinful man." But, knowing how much Christ has suffered and died for us when we were yet sinners, Saint Paul says: "Let us then with confidence draw near to the throne of grace, that we may receive mercy and find grace to help in time of need" (Heb. 4:16). The best way to approach the throne of grace is to go courageously to the Sacrament of Confession.

Courage Creates Greatness

Along with overcoming fear, courage inspires one to do great things. Traditionally known as *magnanimity* (large-souledness) and *magnificence* (splendid nobility), these subvirtues of courage characterize the truly great man. A man with these virtues is self-possessed and unaffected by the opinion of others. He takes delight in helping others, but is at the same time self-reliant. While not lacking in confidence, he is humble and draws attention away from himself. He is generally soft-spoken but is not afraid to lead. This type of man is generous with his resources, especially in the service of the Church. It is this sort of courage that inspired the great men and women of the Church to build great cathedrals and schools and produce works of literature and art. In this respect, we can say courage inspires greatness.

Patience is another subvirtue of courage. Patience enables us to bear affliction without anxiety or discouragement. As Saint Thomas Aquinas says: "A man is said to be patient . . . because of praiseworthy conduct in enduring immediate injuries in such a way as not to be unduly dejected by them."[4] For example, in sickness, or even professional disappointment, patience is needed to keep one from being overly discouraged, or even despairing. Patience is courage borne out over time.

With all the unexpected challenges we face each day, patience is a necessary virtue for the moral life. With the troubles of life, it is tempting to simply give up in despair. But Saint Thomas Aquinas asserts: "Patience is to ensure that we do not abandon virtue's good through a dejection of this kind."[5] Thus, a courage-informed patience helps us to persevere in seeking our own perfection and that of the world. And it is through the exercise of patience that we grow in faith and virtue (Jas. 1:2-4). In addition, it is through patience that we save our souls (cf. Lk. 21:19).

Courageous to the End

Courage also requires that we be ready to die for the sake of what is right. A classic example of this is the story of Eleazar (2 Mac. 18-31). During a pagan persecution of the Jews, an old man, Eleazar, is told to sacrifice to the gods and eat pork, which is forbidden to Jews. The narrative says that Eleazar took courage as men should and refused to break the law of God, even under threat of death and torture. Some of the officials gave Eleazar the option of faking his homage to the gods, but he replied:

> For even if for the present I should avoid the punishment of men, yet whether I live or die I shall not escape the hands of the Almighty. Therefore, by *manfully* giving up my life now, I will

---

[4] *Summa*, IIa IIae, q. 136, art. 4.
[5] *Summa*, IIa IIae, q. 136, art. 4.

show myself worthy of my old age and leave to the young a noble example of how to die a good death willingly and nobly for the revered and holy laws (2 Mac. 6:26-28).

Eleazar is an exceptional model of how even the good of this life must not be held dearer than God and His law.

Our Christian faith makes it clear that we must be willing to die rather than sin. The saints provide us with countless examples of courage, even to the point of death. If it were not for the courage of the early Christians, the Church would not have survived into the third century. It is because of the powerful witness of the early martyrs that Constantine was converted and allowed the faith to be spread throughout the Roman Empire and beyond. It was the courage of the Jesuit and Franciscan missionaries that led them to evangelize the Americas even though they knew that the likelihood of a savage death could well await them. Thus the martyrs, by laying down their lives for Christ and the spread of the Gospel, make the supreme act of courage (cf. Catechism, no. 2473). And today, the courage of the martyrs all over the world still proclaims the beauty of the Gospel in the most powerful way.

Questions

Fortitude is, in a sense, one of the manliest of all the virtues because it reflects the other virtues pushed to their breaking point. Real men will stay the course.

What do the following passages have to say about bravery in the face of suffering?

1. Read 2 Corinthians 4:16-18. What kind of perspective ought we to have?

_____

_____

2. Read 2 Timothy 3:12-15.

a. What are we to expect as followers of Christ?

_____

_____

b. Where can we go to find the encouragement we need?

_____

_____

3. Read 1 Peter 2:21-25. Following Christ's example, what should we do in times of suffering?

_____

_____

4. Read 1 Peter 4:12-16.

a. What should we expect in this life if we follow Christ?

_____

_____

b. What are we to expect in the life to come?

_____

_____

5. According to 2 Timothy 1:7, why are Christian men specifically called to be men of strength?

_____

_____

6. According to Philippians 1:27-29, what is the unique privilege of Christians?

_____

_____

7. Jesus made it clear that following Him would require bravery. What are some practical implications of Our Lord's words in Luke 9:23?

_____

_____

8. Scripture gives us many examples of men who do not possess courage and allow fear to dictate their actions, as well as examples of men who do possess the virtue of courage. The following passages contrast men with and without courage. Look up these passages and determine who does and does not possess courage. How does fear dictate the actions of those without courage?

a. Numbers 13:1–14:10. Note the difference between Joshua and Caleb and the other ten spies who bring an evil report of the Promised Land.

_____

_____

_____

_____

b. 1 Samuel 17:19–25, 32-49. Note how all of the men of Israel, except David, flee from battle against Goliath and the Philistines.

_____

_____

_____

9. Is there a particular challenge in your life that you have been unwilling to confront?

_____

_____

_____

10. What specifically can you do to grow in courage and fortitude?

_____

_____

_____

Memory Verse
"Therefore, since we are surrounded by
so great a cloud of witnesses, let us also lay aside every weight,
and sin which clings so closely, and let us run with perseverance
the race that is set before us, looking to Jesus the pioneer and
perfecter of our faith, who for the joy that was set before him
endured the cross, despising the shame, and is seated
at the right hand of the throne of God."
Hebrews 12:1-2

Chapter 5
Men of Temperance

As a result of the fall of Adam, human nature is weakened and wounded. Thus "man-as-he-is" is not what God originally intended him to be. One of the effects of our wounded nature is what theologians call *concupiscence* (Catechism, no. 1264), which refers to how our passions and desires are not completely and easily subject to reason. This does not mean that we cannot control ourselves at all or that we deny our desires completely. It just means that to attain control of them we must engage in the arduous acquisition of the virtues by the grace of Christ (cf. Catechism, no. 2517). The fact that we are wounded does not mean that we are beyond repair. It simply means that "man-as-he-is" must be renewed in Christ through grace and the virtues to become "man-as-he-ought-to-be," that is, fulfilling his potential as a man of God.

What Is Temperance?

> Temperance is the moral virtue that moderates the attraction of pleasures and provides balance in the use of created goods. It ensures the will's mastery over instincts and keeps desires within the limits of what is honorable (Catechism, no. 1809).

Temperance controls our passions and desires, particularly for food, drink, and sex. These three things are good in themselves, but when they are inordinately pursued they can be very dangerous. Since the pleasure attached to food, drink, and sex are so powerful, we need a strong and disciplined will to moderate them. This power of controlling one's passions and desires for pleasure is found in the virtue of temperance. "Temperance moderates the attraction of the pleasures of the senses and provides balance in the use of created goods" (Catechism, no. 1838). Just as the virtue of courage moderates inordinate fear of pain, temperance moderates the attraction to pleasure. Both virtues are essential for self-control.

Food and alcohol taken in wrong measure are not just unhealthy, but sinful. Gluttony names the vice of immoderate consumption of food and drink. Although our society today looks down on such activity as being unhealthy, this is far from the Christian perspective that calls gluttony one of the seven deadly sins. Overindulgence in such earthly pleasures not only weakens our will, but it also turns our hearts from God and heaven. As a result, our attachments to temporal things increase while our desire for God decreases. Thus Jesus speaks of the seed cast among the thorns as being

> those who hear the word, but the cares of the world, and the delight in riches, and the desire for other things, enter in and choke the word, and it proves unfruitful (Mk. 4:18).

So also the Gospel writers remind us that "where your treasure is, there will your heart be also" (Mt. 6:21).

If the pleasure associated with food and drink is powerful enough to seduce us into abusing them against common sense, how much more is this true regarding sex. Sex is good, but illicit sex is gravely immoral. For this reason, one of the most challenging and important issues in the area of temperance is sex. The specific virtue of temperance that relates to the proper control of our sexual desire is called the virtue of *chastity*. Chastity is a kind of subvirtue of temperance (Catechism, no. 2341). Chastity is the virtue of using sex in the right way. Thus, if one is married, chastity requires that sex be reserved for your spouse alone, carried out in love and openness to life. Openness to life means not using any contraception. Chastity for single people means abstaining from sexual activity, since that is reserved for marriage alone.

Sex and its accompanying desires and passions are not of themselves bad. Indeed, when sex is in the proper context of marriage, it is a great good. God Himself created sex. His first command, telling married couples to "be fruitful and multiply," is given in the first chapter of Genesis! Neither God nor His Church are against sex; it is just the abuse or inappropriate use of sex that is prohibited. Here is an analogy to make the point. Fire of itself is not bad or good, it depends on its context and use. For example, fire in a fireplace is good; it brings both warmth and light to the home. But if the fire is taken out of its proper context, and is sparked in the kitchen or bedroom, the fire does not warm so much as consume and, instead of lighting up the house, it belches out smoke and flame that not only damages but can kill. Fire in a house should be in the fireplace. Sex and sexual passion are like that fire. In the proper context of marriage, like fire in the fireplace, sex is a great good. But taken out of that context, it is a consuming and deadly fire. It does not take much for the sparks of sexual passion to fan into an uncontrollable blaze. In the end, sex outside of marriage is as destructive as a fire, and such fire has ravaged many a home.

The virtue of chastity is a powerful virtue. Chastity empowers us to control and moderate the fire of sexual desire. Once we gain this self-control, we have the freedom to love. For a married man to freely give himself to his spouse in sexual intimacy, he must have the virtue of chastity. Without this virtue, sex simply involves the alleviation of one's sexual desires by which the spouse is used as an object for the sake of one's own desire. But once one has mastery over one's passions, the giving of self is possible. One cannot give what one does not possess. Only the chaste have the ability to give themselves freely in true conjugal love. Having the virtue of chastity makes a dramatic difference in the nature and depth of conjugal love; it is the difference between loving and using.

Unfortunately, our secular culture often views sexual promiscuity as a mark of manhood. This twisted view is far from the truth. To surrender to one's passions and commit sexual sin, especially infidelity to one's wife and family, is not only a shameful crime, but also a mark of profound weakness. The man who surrenders to his passions acts as a pathetic slave to his desires and is far from the real man who has the strength of will to rule his passions. Many forge chains of bondage by allowing their hearts to go out to someone besides their wife. The affection and emotions that arise cause the heart and soul to descend into a terrible fall, one that is much harder to arise from than they ever imagine. Saint Augustine once observed in his *Confessions* that lust served becomes a custom, and custom not resisted becomes a necessity. Saint Augustine well knew how strong the bondage is that accompanies unchaste living. It is not without reason that Scripture warns that sin enslaves.

Chastity is an essential virtue for the Christian life. Thus Saint Paul constantly hammers home the importance of chastity:

> For this is the will of God, your sanctification: that you abstain from immorality; that each one of you know how to control his own body in holiness and honor, not in the passion of lust like heathen who do not know God (1 Thess. 4:3-5).

Saint Paul expects Christians to live differently from the pagan culture around them. Control of one's body is a mark of Christian living, which stands in sharp contrast to the lust that characterizes the life of those who are without God. Saint Paul holds to this so strongly that he often reminds us that those who commit immorality, which includes adultery or fornication, will not, unless they sincerely repent, enter the kingdom of God.

Chastity has made God's top ten list. The Sixth Commandment states, "You shall not commit adultery" (Ex. 20:14). God could not be clearer; fidelity in marriage is crucial to loving and serving God.

We must recognize the beauty and nobility of temperance in all its forms, and the contrasting ugliness and shame when it is absent. To surrender to our base passions is to play the beast. Not only that, giving in to our passions robs us of peace. Peace of soul is a fruit only of those who have conquered themselves. Peace belongs to the victor, not the vanquished. Jesus speaks of the rich reward of chastity in His beatitudes. Our Lord confers this blessing upon the chaste: "Blessed are the pure in heart, for they shall see God" (Mt. 5:8). Purity opens the mind and heart to perceive and see God. Conversely, Saint Thomas Aquinas observed that impurity causes the mind and heart to be darkened.[1]

Curiosity Killed the Cat

To preserve this virtue, it is important to closely guard the senses (cf. Catechism, no. 2520). Curiosity can lead us into temptations to sexual impurity that can bring about our downfall. Take King David as an example. One day, while David had idle time on his hands, he strolled around the roof of his palace. His eyes came upon a beautiful woman bathing on the roof of her own home. Then David made a fatal mistake. Forgetting the Ninth Commandment: "You shall not covet your neighbor's wife" (Ex. 20:17), he kept looking lustfully at the woman. David's desire for her becomes so enkindled that he quickly arranged to commit adultery with her. The bitter fruit of David's lustful glance was adultery. Not without reason does Jesus declare, "every one who looks at a woman lustfully has already committed adultery with her in his heart" (Mt. 5:28). Without custody of eyes, there will not be custody of our passions. The eyes are the portals to the heart; if they are left unchecked, the heart will be like a boat adrift without anchor, thrown about by the violent waves of emotion.

---

[1] For example, see *Summa*, IIa IIae, q. 142, art. 4; IIa IIae, q. 151, art. 4; and IIa IIae, q. 156, art. 2.

Curiosity regarding pornography or improper scenes on TV or the movies, or even the annual swimsuit edition of *Sports Illustrated* magazine can disturb our emotions and enkindle our passions. Saint James warns us:

> [E]ach person is tempted when he is lured and enticed by his own desire. Then desire when it has conceived gives birth to sin; and sin when it is full-grown brings forth death (Jas. 1:14-15).

We must be vigilant in our entertainment choices, especially with respect to TV programs and movies that often exploit women for the sake of ratings and money. It is not a matter of being mature enough to handle the material. If you are a man, then you have hormones, and that means you are wired by nature to get sexually aroused at the sight of a woman's body. It is simply a biological fact that looking upon a scantily dressed woman will usually arouse passion in a man, unless of course he is not made of flesh and blood.

The Power of Passion

Having the virtue of chastity does not numb your passions, it simply means that you keep your sexual passions controlled and lead them to be enkindled only in the context of marital love. Passions of themselves are not bad, but they must be used in the proper way and right context (cf. Catechism, no. 1773). "Emotions and feelings can be taken up into the *virtues* or perverted by the *vices*" (Catechism, no. 1768, original emphasis). Through the virtues, man masters his passions and disposes them toward good things, whereas the man without virtue remains weak and "succumbs to disordered passions and exacerbates them" (*ibid.*).

One must be man enough to know his limitations and avoid the near occasion of sin. This requires the virtue of prudence. Many men have entered into immoral relationships that began as seemingly innocent acquaintances. In modern society, men and women often must work together. The danger of working in such close proximity comes in letting those working relationships develop into something too intimate. This can happen almost imperceptibly, where a friendship slowly grows and the heart becomes emotionally attached. To use a simple analogy, you can put a frog in a pan of water and slowly turn up the temperature by a mere degree at a time and soon the frog will boil to death without ever having perceived the danger until it was too late to jump out. Too often, men enter into imprudent relationships with women, only to realize too late that the temperature has reached the boiling point.

Setting boundaries from the very beginning protects a relationship from becoming more than it should. A good example of this is Joseph of the Old Testament. Joseph was tempted by his boss' wife, who tried to seduce him (Gen. 39). When she found him alone and aggressively came after him, Joseph did what any true and wise man should do—he ran! The fact that Joseph fled does not mean he lacked courage, for courage is facing fear and danger in the right way, and the right way to face temptations of the flesh is to withdraw from them. Joseph would have been imprudent to simply stand his ground in the face of such a direct attack. How many men have fallen into the arms of adultery when they thought they could withstand the temptation. Joseph kept his purity intact because he fled from an occasion of sin. He was wise because he knew his limitations.

Self-Mastery

Having the virtue of chastity means obtaining self-control. One who has temperance is like a king who rules his passions and emotions. Without this virtue, one is effectively a slave to one's passions. The struggle for self-mastery is a dramatic one, but it begins with modest steps. A good exercise is to gain control of one's appetite with food and drink. Disciplining the will to the pleasures of food and drink is a training ground that trains the will to be self-controlled in the face of sexual pleasures. Fasting, as well as abstaining from rich food and drink, is a means of further exercising one's will, putting one's desires into subjection to the will and reason. Many ancient thinkers have seen a relationship between sexual impurity and overindulgence in food and drink. Indeed, most times in the Bible when someone gets drunk, sexual sins often follow. That is why fasting was a penance for adultery in the Middle Ages, because the penance was seen as a way to restore the power of the will to deny inordinate pleasures. All these exercises will help develop control with the sexual appetite and the power to live as masters of the body rather than be its slave.

Saint Paul speaks of the Christian life as a great contest and compares the Christian to the Olympic athlete. Just as the Olympic athlete strives for a crown, Paul says that each Christian must strive for the heavenly reward which only comes to those who achieve self-control:

> Do you not know that in a race all the runners compete, but only one receives the prize? So run that you may obtain it. Every athlete exercises self-control in all things. They do it to receive a perishable wreath, but we an imperishable (1 Cor. 9:24-25).

If athletes make all kinds of sacrifices and demands on their bodies in order to achieve passing fame and honor, how much more should we subdue our bodies for the sake of Christ and eternal glory?

Questions

1. According to Proverbs 25:28, what is the man like who has no self-control?

_____

_____

2. In the struggle to gain self-control, we are not alone. In Galatians 5:22-23, Saint Paul lists the fruits of the Spirit. The Spirit produces these fruits within our soul. What are these fruits? How can we cultivate them in our lives?

_____

_____

_____

_____

3. Note in 2 Peter 1:5-7 how the virtues work together.

a. How do we begin the process?

_____

_____

b. Where in this chain could you use some work?

_____

_____

4. In the parable of the seeds (Mt. 13:1-23), Jesus teaches how the seed is choked by the cares of this world. How does self-control help us to overcome this obstacle?

_____

_____

For the man of God, there are two major areas that require the virtue of temperance, or self-control: sobriety and chastity. Let's examine what the Scriptures have to say about these two important topics:

Sobriety

5. The prophet Isaiah warns us about the party life. From what does it distract us? (See Isaiah 5:11-12.)

_____

_____

6. Saint Paul reminds us that we have been called to follow Jesus Christ. What are some of the fatal distractions he warns us of in Romans 13:11-14?

_____

_____

7. Read Ephesians 5:18-19. Saint Paul contrasts two types of life. What is the meaning of the word "dissipation" or "debauchery"?

_____

_____

_____

Chastity

8. According to 1 Corinthians 6:18-20, why are we to flee immorality?

_____

_____

_____

9. Read Ephesians 5:1-5. As men of God we are called to imitate Him, just as Christ did. What is the certain consequence of unrepentant immorality?

_____

_____

10. Saint Paul calls us to please God "more and more" in our daily lives. Read 1 Thessalonians 4:1-5. What does he say God's will is for us?

_____

_____

11. The Scriptures teach that marriage is sacred. Note the language in Hebrews 13:4. How does this passage describe adultery?

_____

_____

_____

12. What is the secret to Job's ability to be chaste? (See Job 31:1.) What practical steps can we take to do likewise?

_____

_____

_____

13. Do people take sins of the flesh as seriously as Jesus does in Matthew 5:27-30?

_____

_____

_____

14. We live in a culture which says that it is okay to look, but not to touch. Is this a Christ-centered attitude? Why or why not?

_____

_____

_____

15. What is the relevance of Matthew 5:28 to pornography? Why do you think pornography is addictive and sinful?

_____

_____

_____

16. Many excuse their lack of self-control with regard to sexual desire by claiming that their hormones and bodily urges are too strong to not be obeyed. How does this square with Saint Paul's observation in 1 Corinthians 10:13?

_____

_____

Now let's take a look at two biblical examples of how a lack of temperance can lead to destruction. Both David and Solomon were serious about their relationship with God, yet each fell through a lack of self-control.

17. Read 2 Samuel 11.

a. What did David do that led him to commit adultery with Bethsheba?

_____

_____

b. David, who had been a righteous man, went so far to cover up his sin that he killed Bethsheba's husband, Uriah. David probably would not have killed in order to sleep with Bethsheba, but why do you think he was willing to kill in order to cover it up?

_____

_____

c. How is the problem of abortion analogous to David's killing of Uriah?

_____

_____

_____

18. Read 1 Kings 11:1-11. What led Solomon to bring the kingdom of Israel into ruin so quickly?

_____

_____

19. According to Deuteronomy 17:17, could kings of Israel have many wives?

_____

_____

20. Read Proverbs 7. This is a father's warning to his son concerning loose women. How do we heed this advice and teach it to our sons?

_____

_____

21. Another challenge to temperance is obscene language and off-color jokes. What does Saint Paul say about obscene language in 1 Corinthians 15:33-34? How does this relate to off-color humor? (See also Ephesians 5:4.)

_____

_____

_____

22. How can we practically apply Saint Paul's admonition in Romans 8:14 to our entertainment choices, particularly movies and TV?

_____

_____

23. See also Saint Paul's principle for Christian living in Romans 12:1-3 and Philippians 4:6-8. Our minds are somewhat like computers: "Garbage in, garbage out." What practical steps can we take to purify our hearts and thoughts?

_____

_____

There is no time like the present to begin making changes. Can you resolve now to make a commitment to daily prayer? You can begin with five minutes of reading Scripture every day.

24. Read 1 Corinthians 9:24-27.

a. Why does Saint Paul compare spiritual self-mastery to the ordeal of athletics?

_____

_____

b. What does Saint Paul say about himself regarding temperance?

_____

_____

25. Is there an area in your life that calls for more self-control?

_____

_____

26. What can you do today to begin exercising self-control in this area?

_____

_____

_____

Memory Verse
"I appeal to you therefore, brethren,
by the mercies of God,
to present your bodies as a living sacrifice,
holy and acceptable to God,
which is your spiritual worship.
Do not be conformed to this world
but be transformed by the renewal of your mind,
that you may prove what is the will of God,
what is good and acceptable and perfect."
Romans 12:1-2

Chapter 6
Men of Faith

Faith is such an integral part of our daily lives that we usually are not even aware that we operate on faith for some of our most basic activities. When we pick up the phone or jump in the car, we believe these machines will work even though we may not have the most basic understanding of how they work. We believe the car will run properly because we judge the people who built the car to be trustworthy. When we board a plane, we may not know anything about aeronautical engineering, but we trust that the engineers who built the plane know it well. Supernatural faith is a similar trust, except that the person in whom we place our trust happens to be God, who can neither deceive nor be deceived.

If we want to better understand the supernatural virtue of faith, there is no better place to start than with the definition given to us in Sacred Scripture: "Faith is the assurance of things hoped for, the conviction of things not seen" (Heb. 11:1). Note the key terms, *assurance* and *conviction*. At the same time, however, faith is belief in what is *hoped for* and *not seen*. It is a striking paradox that faith has such solid assurance and certain conviction when it is based on hope for something not present and something real but unseen. A paradox, however, is very different from a contradiction.

The Catechism has much to say about faith. Building on the wisdom of Saint Thomas Aquinas, the Catechism gives a penetrating analysis of what faith is:

In faith, the human intellect and will cooperate with divine grace: "Believing is an act of the intellect assenting to the divine truth by command of the will moved by God through grace" (Catechism, no. 155).[1]

This is a mouthful, so let's try to unpack it.

Faith and Reason

The human soul has two basic faculties: the power to know, the intellect, and the power to choose, the will. Normally, the intellect presents something to the will for it to choose. For example, the intellect judges that it is better to stay away from the edge of a cliff. The will, seeing this as a good thing, directs the body to keep a safe distance from the edge. In faith, however, rather than the intellect directing the will, the will directs the intellect. The will, choosing to follow the direction of another authority, moves the intellect to accept something as true even though the mind does not yet see it to be true. This is not to say, as we shall see, that the mind is forced to accept something it sees to be false. The intellect accepts something to be true that surpasses, not contradicts, its power to know. As such, we can say faith is a virtue of the intellect.

All of this is powered by the grace of God. Grace is the free gift of God infused into the soul, elevating the powers of the soul to participate in the divine life of the Trinity. In supernatural faith, grace raises the mind to receive truth that would otherwise be unattainable. We cannot know that God is Trinity without the direct act of God revealing this truth to us. We see, then, that supernatural faith is dependent upon God's free movement of Himself to us. In turn, faith is a response to God's action. "Faith is a personal adherence of the whole man to God who reveals himself. It involves an assent of the intellect and will to the self-revelation God has made through his deeds and words" (Catechism, no. 176).

---

[1] Quoting *Summa*, IIa IIae, q. 2, art. 9.

Faith does not contradict what we are able to know through our own natural powers of reason. Pope John Paul II has written extensively, especially in his encyclical *Fides et Ratio*, about the relationship of reason and faith. Human reason prepares a foundation on which faith rises. The two are essentially and necessarily united. Reason prepares the way for faith and faith elevates and perfects reason. We do not live by blind faith. Faith does not suspend reason, but rather it engages reason. Although it may go beyond reason, faith never goes against it. The two, faith and reason, complement each other. They are, as Pope John Paul II has said, the two wings by which the mind ascends to God.

In this complementary relationship, reason prepares the person for faith but also seeks to understand faith. This is what we call theology. Theology is *faith seeking understanding*. Through a careful study of Revelation, we are able to grow in our understanding of God and His plan of salvation. Authentic theology, then, requires the theologian to be a person of faith. As we approach God as students of Revelation, we should always come to the subject with an attitude of prayer and humility. As one theologian has said, "theology should be done on one's knees."

The difficulty of faith is not in its object, God, but rather its subject, the person who must put faith into practice. Supernatural faith can vary in degrees because each individual has a different level of faith. The amount of trust one places in God can vary widely. This is where the element of virtue is crucial to understanding what faith is and how it works. It is often thought that faith is simply the mind assenting to something. A classic example is the question, "Do you believe in God?" Often the assumption is that faith is only a matter of intellectual affirmation of God's existence. Thus faith becomes merely the acceptance of a proposition. But faith is a much richer reality than the intellectual "downloading" of an idea. Faith is not just a matter of the mind, but also a habit of the heart (cf. Catechism, no. 1814). It is not enough to believe that God exists—the demons do this and tremble (Jas. 2:19)—rather, it is a matter of trusting in the goodness of the One who is. This trust takes an act of the will, in cooperation with the mind. The fact that faith includes both the heart and the head is why it is a virtue.

Increase Our Faith

Jesus recognized the varying degrees of faith possessed among the people He encountered. He was amazed that the centurion, who trusted in the power of Jesus' word to heal, had such great faith (Mt. 8:10). The woman who was healed simply by touching Jesus' robe is told that it was her faith that made her well (Mk. 5:34). In contrast, Jesus often chides the disciples as "men of little faith" (Mt. 8:26). And back in His hometown Jesus is unable to do mighty deeds because of the people's unbelief (Mk. 5:5-6). If faith is a matter of simple intellectual assent, how could there be such varying degrees of faith, from little to great, in Jesus' estimation? For if faith is simply assent to a proposition, like 2+2=4, then one would either have it or not; it would not be possessed in varying degrees. But since faith requires the assent of the will in addition to the mind, as explained above, faith can vary because the will to trust can vary widely between strong and wavering. To have strong faith takes a habitual disposition of the will to cooperate with God's grace. The virtue of faith, like all other virtues, only comes at the price of habitual effort and willing.

A classic example from Scripture that illustrates the nature of faith is the story of the twelve spies. When Israel approached the Promised Land, while they were still in the wilderness, Moses sent out twelve spies to scout out the land that flowed with milk and honey, the land Israel was called to conquer. Moses charged the spies to bring back a report, and as he sent them off he exhorted them saying, "Be of good courage" (Num. 13:20). At the end of forty days, the spies returned from their mission. The camp was full of anticipation and interest in what news the spies would bring back. The spies reported how good the land was, but then ten of the spies reported that their enemies were too strong for them. Israel was outnumbered and outgunned, the cities were well fortified, and the bottom line was that Israel did not have any chance of defeating the Canaanites. This, they claimed, was mission impossible. The news caused the people of Israel to lose heart, and they soon began talk of returning to Egypt (cf. Num. 14:1-3).

Two of the spies, however, challenged the majority report. Joshua and Caleb spoke before the people and Moses and argued that the mission was not impossible. Yet they did not disagree with the details of the majority report, just its conclusion. For Joshua and Caleb did not disagree with anything the other spies reported; yes, it was true they faced a powerful enemy. But they were not in this alone: God was on their side. Joshua's point was to have faith in God:

> Only, do not rebel against the LORD; and do not fear the people of the land, for they are bread for us; their protection is removed from them, and the LORD is with us; do not fear them (Num. 14:9).

Joshua made it clear that his confidence was not in Israel's strength, but in the Lord's.

The people refused to heed Joshua's advice, and they began to call for Joshua and Caleb to be stoned. Then the glory of the Lord appeared, and God said, "[H]ow long will they not believe in me, in spite of all the signs which I have wrought among them?" (Num. 14:11). Israel's failure was a failure to trust in God. As a result that generation was then condemned to spend forty years in the wilderness, in atonement for the forty days the spies scouted out the land in disbelief.

Israel had a God-given vocation to take the Promised Land. They looked at what they were called to do and complained that it was impossible. Often God calls us to do more than is humanly possible, but He never leaves us to do it alone. "For with God nothing will be impossible" (Lk. 1:37). All we need to do is put our trust in Our Heavenly Father, and then work as hard as we can. No matter how weak we may feel, we must remember the Lord's words to Saint Paul, "My grace is sufficient for you, for my power is made perfect in weakness" (2 Cor. 12:9).

Supernatural Perspective

Supernatural faith, however, takes more than human willing, it takes divine grace. This is why faith is called a theological virtue. The Church recognizes three theological virtues: faith, hope, and love. By "theological" the Church simply means that these virtues are on a higher level than the natural virtues, because they have God as their origin, motive, and object (Catechism, no. 1812). Man apart from God cannot attain the theological virtues, nor does God give them apart from human cooperation. These virtues require human willing and habit, just as the natural virtues, but they also require God's grace to empower the human willing. Why? Because the theological virtues demand far more than human nature can accomplish on its own. The virtues perfect our human nature, but the theological virtues go a step further and elevate human nature to a participation in the divine nature and life of God (Catechism, no. 1813).

An example of the difference between natural and supernatural faith will help clarify this distinction. One may say, "have no fear, trust in God." But a reply may be made that many evil things happen to good people. A good example is the tragedy of the Egyptian plane crash, Flight 990. The people on board were innocent. Indeed, one family with young children on that fateful flight were Christian missionaries heading to Africa. They exemplify the reality that bad things can and do happen to good people. So, how can one put fear aside by having faith in God? The mysterious answer, to borrow the words of Job, is "though he slay me, yet I will trust in him" (Job 13:15, KJV). Trusting in God in the midst of tragedy and death, as Job did, goes far beyond the limits of natural faith. For natural faith looks to the things of this world and no further. Thus death puts a finite limit to the realm of natural faith, but supernatural faith remains unconquered by death, knowing that death does not have the last word.

Christians believe that death, in the end, is overcome by life. Faith in the death and Resurrection of Jesus leads Christians to hope that God will, in the end, right all wrongs and vindicate the just. Thus the theological virtue of faith empowers us to have a supernatural outlook on life, which relativizes our worldly fears and gives us an eternal perspective. This is the perspective that the martyrs, the greatest witnesses of faith, demonstrate. Thus Saint Maximilian Kolbe and Saint Edith Stein did not lose faith in the midst of the Nazi death camps during the Holocaust, even when the time for their deaths came. They had the theological virtue of faith, which empowered them to say, "Though he slay me, yet I will trust in him."

Reach for the Stars

The patriarch Abraham exemplified the supernatural element of faith, which is why he is often called the "father of faith." After Abraham had exhibited tremendous faith in answering God's call to abandon his homeland and come to a new, "promised land," Abraham met other trials. The largest trial was his and Sarah's infertility; they were getting old and were childless. One day, when God promised to give Abraham a "great reward," Abraham asked God a sharply pointed question. What, Abraham wanted to know, was the good of all the material blessings that God was bestowing on an old man, since he remained childless (Gen. 15:1-3)? All the good things of the world mean nothing without someone with whom to share them. God responded by bringing Abraham outside the tent and asking him a question, "Look toward heaven, and number the stars, if you are able to number them" (Gen. 15:5). Then God declared to Abraham that his descendents would be like the number of the stars. "And he believed the LORD; and he reckoned it to him as righteousness" (Gen. 15:6). Abraham believed, in spite of the empirical evidence that shouted out how impossible it was for an elderly couple to conceive.

One key aspect of Abraham's faith in this story can be easily missed. When God pulled Abraham outside the tent, what time was it? We immediately think that the question of "numbering the stars if you can" relates to the infinite number of stars. This is especially tempting for us, as we moderns have high-tech telescopes that give us incredible pictures of the vastness of the universe. But this is far from the narrator's point in Genesis. For it was not dark when Abraham and God had their conversation outside the nomad's tent. For later in the story we are told that the sun sets (Gen. 15:12). Thus, when this conversation about stars took place, it was the middle of a hot day in the Middle East. God's question then takes on a new twist. "Count the stars if you can" is not about numbering a vast host, but seeing past the dazzling sun. Abraham couldn't see a single star, just as he couldn't see a single descendent. And this was exactly God's point. God was saying to Abraham, you cannot see the stars now, but I can, and likewise, you cannot see your descendents now, but I can; and they are as plentiful as the stars in the heavens. Abraham got God's point. He did not have the power of sight to see the stars nor his future family, but God did, and that was enough.

Abraham trusted God with his will, even though his intellect did not understand.

> No distrust made him waver concerning the promise of God, but he grew strong in his faith as he gave glory to God, fully convinced that God was able to do what he had promised (Rom. 4:20-21).

At times trusting God is an act of the will, which commands the mind to assent and to trust. Like Abraham, we often must walk by faith, not by sight.

The Christian faith does not stand in fear of death, for it believes in the One who has gone through death to the other side, Jesus Christ. Through His death and Resurrection we have faith, a faith that inspires in us a love that is stronger than death (Song 8:6).

Question

1. According to Hebrews 11:6, why is faith so important?

_____

_____

2. Read Romans 5:8 and Ephesians 2:8-9. Is our salvation based upon our works, or upon God's free and undeserved gift?

_____

_____

3. According to Jesus (Mt. 16:15-17), how did Peter know Jesus was the Christ?

_____

_____

The salvation offered by Jesus Christ is a free and undeserved gift. By Christ's free gift of His life, death on the Cross, and Resurrection, He has won salvation for each of us.

Our justification comes from the grace of God. Grace is *favor*, the *free* and *undeserved help* that God gives us to respond to his call to become children of God, adoptive sons, partakers of the divine nature and of eternal life (Catechism, no. 1996, original emphasis; cf. Jn. 1:12-18; 17:3; Rom. 8:14-17; 2 Pet. 1:3-4).

4. According to Colossians 2:12-14, why is it impossible for us to merit faith?

_____

_____

5. We are dead in our sins and unable to save ourselves. Read Romans 4:1-3. What is the effect of Abraham's faith?

_____

_____

6. In our culture when we hear the word "faith," it's often used in weak statements such as "just have a little faith." What words does Hebrews 11:1 use to describe faith?

_____

_____

As with the other theological virtues, faith has two aspects: First, how we get it, and second, what we are supposed to do with it. We gain the theological virtues as free and undeserved gifts of God, but we must live them once we have them.

7. Remember that Ephesians 2:8-9 stressed that faith was a gift and could not be earned. According to Ephesians 2:10, why are we to do good works once we have faith?

_____

_____

8. Read Matthew 22:1-14.

a. Did the wedding guests deserve (merit) their invitation to the feast?

_____

_____

b. What happened to the guest who arrived inappropriately dressed?

_____

_____

9. According to Saint Paul (1 Cor. 13:2), what is the value of faith without love?

_____

_____

10. Read James 2:14-23.

a. What is faith without works? _____

b. Once we have received faith, how is it perfected?

_____

_____

11. Read Luke 6:45-49. Does Jesus really expect us to do as He says? _____

If we are going to be godly men, we must resolve, "Jesus Christ is either Lord of all or He is not Lord at all."

12. Imagine that Christ asked you the same question, "Why do you call me 'Lord, Lord,' and do not do what I say?" How would you react?

_____

_____

13. What can we do to allow Christ to be the Lord of our lives?

_____

_____

Growing in Faith

14. We must nourish the faith we have been given. According to the following passages, Christ has given us the Church and, through the Church, the Scriptures to guide us in forming our faith:

a. John 17:17. Who guarantees the truth?

_____

_____

b. 1 Timothy 3:14-15. What is the pillar of truth?

_____

_____

c. 2 Timothy 3:14-17. Why should we deepen our knowledge of Scripture?

_____

_____

Over and over again the Scriptures challenge us to be men of virtue. But we need God's assistance. If we truly desire to become men of God, we must be men of prayer.

15. If we desire faith, or to increase our faith, what does Saint John instruct us to do in 1 John 5:14-15?

_____

_____

16. Read Luke 10:16. Can a man believe in Jesus and reject the Church He founded?

_____

_____

One specific way to increase your faith is through prayer. Can you make the time this week to include this brief prayer in your daily prayer time?

Act of Faith
O my God, I firmly believe that You are one God in three divine Persons, Father, Son and Holy Spirit; I believe that Your divine Son became man and died for our sins, and that He will come to judge the living and the dead. I believe these and all the truths which the holy Catholic Church teaches, because You have revealed them, who can neither deceive nor be deceived. Amen.

Memory Verse
"Now faith is the assurance of things hoped for,
the conviction of things not seen."
Hebrews 11:1

Chapter 7

__Men of Hope__

The virtue of hope moves us toward the achievement of something that is challenging, but possible—either on our own power or with another's help. As a theological virtue, hope is an expectation, with the help of God's grace, of eternal happiness.

> Hope is the theological virtue by which we desire the kingdom of heaven and eternal life as our happiness, placing our trust in Christ's promises and relying not on our own strength, but on the help of the grace of the Holy Spirit (Catechism, no. 1817).

Hope is a bridge between the other two theological virtues, faith and love. In the previous chapter, we read that faith is "the *assurance* of things hoped for, the *conviction* of things not seen" (Heb. 11:1). By faith we believe in God, and through love we desire to be with God. Hope is the conviction that what we love through faith will be possessed. Implicit in this definition is the fact that we have not yet reached our destination. Hope looks to the future. The man of hope knows he is not yet where he wants to be, but knows he is on the way. Hope allows us to strive with confidence and expectation toward the future good of final happiness: heaven (cf. Catechism, no. 1024). By anticipating that which is not yet, hope sustains and perfects faith and love in this life. It is the Christian, and only the Christian, who can say, "in the end it will turn out well for me."

Fulfilling Our Desires

Let's look at an example to help illustrate the function of hope. Planning a vacation to Hawaii takes several things. First, it is necessary to believe that Hawaii actually exists (faith). If I did not believe Hawaii existed, planning a trip there would be foolish. Second, I have to want to go there (love). If I hated tropical islands, I would not desire to go to Hawaii. Finally, in order for me to actually make the effort to plan the trip, I have to trust that my efforts to save money, make plans, and get on an airplane will actually get me to Hawaii (hope). Hope, therefore, presumes a belief in the object (faith) and a desire for it (love). We believe in God and heaven, and desire to possess them. Hope is the virtue that connects the two.

Faith itself must be accompanied by hope and love, for alone it loses its power. Saint James gives an example of the futility of faith without hope and love. The demons, who have no hope of salvation, still believe there is a God, but their belief does not lead to faithfulness and love. "You believe that God is one; you do well. Even the demons believe—and shudder" (Jas. 2:19). A life that lacks hope will lead to ruin. Jesus has warned us that if we desire to be a disciple we must take up our cross (cf. Mt. 10:38). Without the hope of salvation, the cost of Christian discipleship is too great. Why would we make sacrifices if we did not have the hope of eternal salvation?

We must remember that hope, as a theological virtue, is the fruit of God's grace. Hope causes us to trust in the mercy of God that, despite our sins and weaknesses, we may experience the joys of heaven. Our hope is rooted in God Himself—in His loving action in our lives and His desire to save us. When we place too much trust in ourselves, or overexaggerate God's mercy to the detriment of our need to cooperate with grace, we tend toward *presumption* (Catechism, no. 2092). Presumption is an unjustified anticipation of the fulfillment of hope.

Presumption is an error that appears in many hidden forms today. The most obvious is the "nice guy" approach to salvation.

As long as I do not do anything mean to people around me and once in awhile do some kind act, I will go to heaven. Religion is not needed and, in fact, often gets in the way. Presumption lures you into believing that you will obtain Christ's mercy and eternal life regardless of how you respond to His challenge to follow Him. It leaves any real effort to pursue holiness meaningless and unnecessary. If I believe that I have already crossed the finish line—or if I believe that all the participants win the same prize— why would I keep running?

The other vice opposing hope is *despair*. Despair belittles Christ's mercy and makes us feel as though we are not worthy of God's forgiveness, that somehow we have "out-sinned" Christ's forgiveness (cf. Catechism, no. 2091). A person who gives into despair will stop seeking God's forgiveness and stop pursuing godly actions because he believes that nothing will help him experience the love and forgiveness of Christ. Despair is in direct opposition to hope and renders faith sterile. If I believe there is a heaven, but I despair of ever getting there, then I will neither try to take the steps that lead to salvation nor cry out for God's assistance. For the Christian, despair is especially damaging since it is a decision against Christ and His gift of redemption.

Despair is one of the most dangerous sins. It attacks man's will to work out his salvation, or even to take on the challenges of another day (cf. Phil. 2:12). It could be said that we have developed a culture of despair in this country, given the pervading presence of hopelessness. The rise of depression, drug abuse, and suicide, especially among young people, is a direct result of this lack of hope. Hope, therefore, is the quiet virtue that needs to be re-discovered and celebrated, for when a person begins to despair, the most terrible consequences are possible.

Running the Race

Imagine life as a marathon. The man who has despaired would refuse to train because he would think it was hopeless and no amount of training could change the outcome. The man with presumption would also refuse to train because he would think training was not necessary. Both are destined to fail. But, the man with hope would train hard because he believed that, although he may not presently be in shape to finish the race, through rigorous training he could become so. Because of this fundamental difference in approach, based upon the hope of success, he would gain the stamina and strength he needs to run the race. Saint Paul uses this very example to stress the importance of a rigorous spiritual life:

> Do you not know that in a race all the runners compete, but only one receives the prize? So run that you may obtain it. Every athlete exercises self-control in all things. They do it to receive a perishable wreath, but we an imperishable. Well, I do not run aimlessly, I do not box as one beating the air; but I pommel my body and subdue it, lest after preaching to others I myself should be disqualified (1 Cor. 9:24-27).

Because of hope, we are able to endure difficulties with joy. And because of hope we are motivated to love God and to follow Him. Life is a marathon, and in the midst of life we can sometimes become discouraged over our failings and disheartened over the challenges of life. Hope provides us with a purpose in life. For the Christian, hope is not some weak experience of positive thinking. Hope is the rock-solid trust that if we cling to Christ and seek His forgiveness, He will always prove Himself faithful to His promises. The hope of heaven can strengthen us in times of suffering. When the Christian martyrs are tortured for their faith, the hope of heaven and of being with the Lord gives them the strength to endure.

Our Christian faith enables us to be joyful in the midst of suffering and hardship. This is because the Christian knows that, despite the present problems, there is a future glory that awaits us (cf. Rom. 8:18). In other words, we may be two touchdowns behind, but we know that through Christ we are ultimately going to triumph. We can be saddened at the present evils and difficulties that we and those we love must endure, but this sadness is tempered by our knowledge that, in the end, God will make all things right. For in the end "he will wipe away every tear from their eyes, and death shall be no more, neither shall there be mourning nor crying nor pain any more, for the former things have passed away" (Rev. 21:4).

It is just such a hope that buoyed Saint Paul's spirits while he was in chains in a dark prison cell because of his faith in Jesus Christ. One of Paul's most cheerful letters is to the Philippians, which he wrote from prison. The tone and theme of the letter is joy. Despite Paul's chains he can say:

> Yes, and I shall rejoice . . . as it is my eager expectation and hope that I shall not be at all ashamed, but that with full courage now as always Christ will be honored in my body, whether by life or by death. For to me to live is Christ, and to die is gain (Phil. 1:19-21).

Saint Paul trusted in God, and he knew well that the final goal was heaven. That is why he could say that although he had suffered the loss of all things, he counted them as refuse compared to the glory that awaited him at the end (cf. Phil. 3:8). If we take our eyes off of the final prize, then we can easily lose the desire that hope enkindles in us. If we lose our desire for heavenly glory, we will sink into the pursuit of earthly goods that are poor counterfeits of the eternal; they are mere trinkets compared to the glorious reward that awaits those who hope for heaven. As Saint Peter says:

> By his great mercy we have been born anew to a living hope through the resurrection of Jesus Christ from the dead, and to an inheritance which is imperishable, undefiled, and unfading, kept in heaven for you, who by God's power are guarded through faith for a salvation ready to be revealed in the last time (1 Pet. 1:3-4).

The Road to Glory

Oddly enough, the virtue of hope shows itself in the midst of hopeless circumstances. It is in the midst of trials and ordeals that we need the theological virtue, the God-given power of hope. Jesus is our model. In the midst of apparent hopelessness, He shows us how to trust in God. From the Cross, Our Lord cried out, "My God, my God, why hast thou forsaken me?" (Mt. 27:46). In this apparent cry of despair, Jesus invites us to search deeper into His thoughts. It is vital that we understand that Jesus' words are taken from the first line of Psalm 22. Jesus' use of this psalm is intentional: He intends to invoke not just the opening line, but the entire psalm. This becomes clear as we realize that there is a striking parallel between the psalmist and Jesus; both are enduring horrific suffering while their oppressors mock them.

Jesus on the Cross makes the lament of Psalm 22 His own. "[T]hey have pierced my hands and my feet," and "they divide my garments among them and for my raiment they cast lots" (Ps. 22:16, 18). Despite his sufferings, the psalmist confesses his trust in God: "In thee our fathers trusted; they trusted, and thou didst deliver them" (v. 4). He then concludes his lament by asserting that God has not abandoned him, "For he has not despised or abhorred the affliction of the afflicted; and he has not hid his face from him, but has heard, when he cried to him" (v. 24). The psalm continues as a song of deliverance. Christ's very point is to show that even when all seems hopeless, when God appears to be far away, even then He is worthy of our trust.

Christ's final words also give this message. "Father, into thy hands I commit my spirit!" (Lk. 23:46). This too is a quote taken from one of the psalms. It is Psalm 31, where the psalmist suffers much in the same way that Jesus did, and yet he concludes his lament with a hope-formed faith: "I had said in my alarm, 'I am driven far from thy sight.' But thou didst hear my supplications, when I cried to thee for help" (Ps. 31:22). Jesus' words are taken from the sacred songs of Israel, songs of lamentation and suffering. Yet these psalms also manifest hope in God, who does not despise the afflictions of His sons.

Thus Saint Paul can speak in his Letter to the Romans about the "hope of sharing the glory of God" (Rom. 5:2). But this hope is forged through the Cross, as Saint Paul goes on to describe:

> More than that, we rejoice in our sufferings, knowing that suffering produces endurance, and endurance produces character, and character produces hope, and hope does not disappoint us, because God's love has been poured into our hearts through the Holy Spirit who has been given to us (Rom. 5:3-5).

The virtue of hope is refined through the crucible of trials and suffering, but the more we persevere through life's challenges, the more we learn that hope "does not disappoint us."

You Haven't Got a Prayer Without Hope

Since we carry this treasure of grace in earthen vessels, it is easy to let our hope leak out: This often happens over time, almost imperceptibly. How do we guard against a loss of Christian hope? The best way is through prayer. Prayer, itself, is a form of hope. Prayer, in one of its most basic forms, is a petition to God. Prayer voices our hope in God's response to our needs. "The Holy Spirit . . . teaches us to pray in *hope*. Conversely, the prayer of the Church and personal prayer nourish hope in us" (Catechism, no. 2657, original emphasis). In voicing our desires to God, we remind ourselves of God's goodness and His desire to give us what we need. Prayer is an exercise of hope and, as such, a guardian of hope, and by practicing and deepening prayer we can strengthen the virtue of hope.

Questions

1. The virtue of hope is the second of the three theological virtues. Read Romans 5:1-5. How does hope relate to faith and love?

_____

_____

2. According to Ephesians 2:12-13, do we have hope without Christ? _____

3. According to Matthew 24:13, what is necessary for salvation?

_____

_____

4. The knowledge that, if we endure until the end, we will be saved may give us some reason for hope. But read 2 Corinthians 12:9. Is there a greater reason for hope?

_____

_____

5. Persevering to the end will not be easy. Yet, in light of the difficulties, how does 1 Corinthians 10:13 help us to have a confident hope in obtaining our eternal reward?

_____

_____

6. Read Titus 3:4-7. We can have great confidence in God's future mercy when we call to mind how He has blessed us in the past. What are some of the reasons for hope offered in this passage?

_____

_____

_____

7. Saint Paul encourages us to be hopeful in Romans 8:18-28. According to this passage, what is the appropriate attitude for us to have when confronting suffering?

_____

_____

8. Scripture tells us about life in heaven in Revelation 21:1-7. How does this vision of our eventual home help us to be hopeful now?

_____

_____

9. According to the following passages, what is the basis of our hope?

a. Romans 8:14-17. What does it mean to be an heir of God?

_____

_____

b. Galatians 4:4-7. What is our relationship with God?

_____

_____

c. 1 John 3:1-3. As great as being a child of God is, what does Scripture tell us that we shall be?

_____

_____

10. Scripture is clear that, in Christ, we are sons of God. Read Matthew 7:7-11. Why can we trust Our Heavenly Father to bless us and lead us to eternal life?

_____

_____

11. Read John 14:1-6. What has Jesus promised us?

_____

_____

12. According to Hebrews 10:19-24, why can we trust Jesus Christ to guide us through this life into heaven?

_____

_____

13. According to John 3:16-17, why did Jesus come into the world?

_____

_____

14. How does Hebrews 6:19 describe our hope in Christ?

_____

_____

15. According to Luke 1:37, how capable is God of leading us to salvation?

_____

_____

16. Given the fact that God has offered us His only Son, how confident ought we to be in His mercy? (See Philippians 1:6.)

_____

_____

17. According to 1 Corinthians 15:3-8, 12-22, what is the reason for our trust that Jesus will come again to lead us to heaven?

_____

_____

18. Read 2 Maccabees 6.

a. How are hope and manliness lived out in the life of Eleazer?

_____

_____

b. How can we learn from his example?

_____

_____

19. Are there specific areas where we can stand up against our culture and bear witness to the hope that is in us?

_____

_____

_____

We can and should ask God to increase our hope. Here is the Act of Hope, which can be a great tool in your personal prayer life.

Act of Hope

O my God, relying on Your infinite goodness and promises, I hope to obtain pardon of my sins, the help of Your grace, and life everlasting, through the merits of Jesus Christ, my Lord and Redeemer. Amen.

Memory Verse

"For I know the plans I have for you,
says the LORD, plans for welfare and not for evil,
to give you a future and a hope."
Jeremiah 29:11

Chapter 8

Men of Love

We now finish with the capstone of all the virtues, love. "And above all these put on love, which binds everything together in perfect harmony" (Col. 3:14). As the Catechism says, "Charity is superior to all the virtues" (Catechism, no. 1826). Most of us are aware that love, sometimes referred to as charity, has priority in the life of a Christian, but the question remains: What is love? "Charity is the theological virtue by which we love God above all things for his own sake, and our neighbor as ourselves for the love of God" (Catechism, no. 1822).

There is much confusion surrounding "love" because we can mean so many things with the same word. I love chocolate. I love my dog. I love my car. I love my kids. I love you. Because the word "love" is used so commonly, it can easily be reduced to emotional sentiment, as if love simply means wanting to kiss somebody. And yet we know that charity requires us to love everyone. We obviously do not, and cannot, desire to kiss everyone. So, what kind of love are we called to?

A Matter of the Will

Love, as a theological virtue, is an act of the will. "To love is to will the good of another" (Catechism, no. 1766).[1] Earlier, we saw how faith is a virtue of the intellect. Love, on the other hand, is a virtue of the will. That is, love is a mode of willing. By willing, we mean choosing something as good. We all love: It is just a question of what do we love—what do we choose as being good for us? The theological virtue of love is the desire for the

---

[1] Cf. *Summa*, Ia IIae, q. 26, art. 4.

greatest good for others and ourselves. The greatest good, of course, is God Himself.

Understanding love as an act of the will is in stark contrast to the more common consideration of love as a feeling. Saint Thomas Aquinas distinguished the passion or feeling of love from love as a virtue. As a passion, love is the desire for some good, like ice cream, baseball, or a Mercedes-Benz. Love, in this sense, is something that happens to us. We are passive recipients of emotional experiences. Our passions, that is, our desires, control our feelings and, in a sense, hold us captive to our basic instincts (cf. Catechism, no. 1765). Although these passions may be good and directed toward a real good, they do not indicate the presence of the virtue of love. Love, as a virtue, is about what we choose, not how we feel.

For example, when a young man commits himself to a woman in the Sacrament of Marriage, he makes a vow to love her regardless of his feelings. What does this mean? As time passes and the trials of life weigh down, the couple may not feel the sentiments of love. Because many people have a wrong understanding of love, they feel justified to leave the marriage and look for those same feelings in another person. This makes sense if we reduce love to mere feelings. True marital love, however, understands that the commitment transcends subjective feelings. The feelings may have been necessary at the beginning of courtship, but if it evolves into true love, feelings become secondary. Marriage is about a choice to commit one's life to another for their well-being regardless of emotions. This is sometimes very difficult, but it is an example of the self-sacrificing nature of love.

Love, in this sense, is not about the wants of the one who loves, but about what is best for the beloved. True love is about the other, not the self. Consequently, love often demands sacrificing one's own desires for the good of the other. The degree to which one is able to sacrifice for others is the measure of his love. We may want to love, but if we are going to will to love, we must have the virtues. The father who rises in the middle of the night to care for his new child is not acting out of a desire to get less sleep (hardly!), but out of love for his new daughter and tired wife. He acts for the benefit of others, not for himself.

There is a wonderful story told of a little boy who worked hard to earn enough money for a beautiful model of a sailing ship. He worked for days to build the ship and finally it was completed. He went down to a local park and placed his beloved ship in the lake. It was a great success and his ship floated perfectly. The model sails even caught the wind and moved the ship along. Then, unexpectedly, a strong gust of wind came and blew the small ship beyond the reach of the boy. He watched helplessly as the wind pulled the ship farther and farther into the great lake. He waited for hours hoping his ship would come back, but it was hopeless. His beloved ship was lost.

Devastated, the boy returned home without his prized possession. Weeks passed and he could not get the ship out of his mind. One day, he was walking through town, and as he passed a local shop, he raised his eyes and could not believe what he saw. His ship was sitting in the storefront window. He rushed in and explained to the owner that the ship was his and how he had lost it. The owner was moved, but he told the boy that he had purchased the ship from the person who found it and that he would have to sell the ship to the boy for a price. Having spent all of his money on the original purchase, the boy went home and began working diligently to save the money he needed to buy back his ship. Finally, with the money in his hand, he returned to the shop and bought his cherished ship. As he held the ship in his hands, the shopkeeper overheard the boy say, "My little ship! How I love you. You are now mine twice. I made you, and then I lost you, but I have bought you back."

In Christ, God has done even more for us! He has created us out of love, and bought us back at the price of His own blood.

Gift of Self

Now we have reached the profound importance of Christianity. In Jesus Christ, we come to know the fullness of truth about God and about love. Saint John the Apostle was known as the "beloved disciple" because of the great love Jesus had shown for him. John gives us the simple truth: "God is love" (1 Jn. 4:8). Jesus shows us the depths of God's love and calls us to imitate Him. True love gives itself for the sake of the other and seeks nothing in return. God is the fullness of love, indeed, the source of all love. God created us to share His love and life with us. Our creation was a free act of God's love. We may think that God created us to bring Himself glory or to get something for Himself, but God was already infinitely and perfectly glorious and happy before He created us. God will be no more glorious or happy after all of history has run its course than He was prior to creation.

> St. Bonaventure explains that God created all things "not to increase his glory, but to show it forth and to communicate it," for God has no other reason for creating than his love and goodness (Catechism, no. 293).

God's love is manifested in our creation, but all the more His love is beautifully revealed in our Redemption, through the life, death and Resurrection of Jesus. Jesus stands to gain nothing for Himself, but love leads Him to pour Himself out for us. Saint Paul writes beautifully of the love of Christ:

> Have this mind among yourselves, which was in Christ Jesus, who though he was in the form of God, did not count equality with God a thing to be grasped, but emptied himself, taking the form of a servant, being born in the likeness of men. And being found in human form he humbled himself and became obedient unto death, even death on a cross (Phil. 2:5-8).

The eternal Son lived in perfect glory and happiness, and yet for the sake of love He became man. Think of what He gave up! And He had nothing to gain personally, rather He did it for love of His Father and for us. This is why Saint Paul writes, "But God shows his love for us in that while we were yet sinners Christ died for us" (Rom. 5:8).

Christian love is aided by the grace of God given to us in the Holy Spirit. From the grace of our Baptism, we are empowered to share in the love of the Trinity. The Catechism teaches that God is an eternal exchange of love (no. 221). Jesus has called each of us to live in that love (cf. 1 Jn. 3). This unique love is the heart of Christian life. Saint Paul's First Letter to the Corinthians offers us a blueprint of Christian love:

> Love is patient and kind; love is not jealous or boastful; it is not arrogant or rude. Love does not insist on its own way; it is not irritable or resentful; it does not rejoice at wrong, but rejoices in the right. Love bears all things, believes all things, hopes all things, endures all things (1 Cor. 13:4-7).

Clearly, love is not about seeking personal satisfaction.

Jesus reveals the depth of God's love from the Cross. In heaven, the Son has eternally poured Himself out in love for the Father. Once the Son takes flesh, Jesus continues to do as a man what He has always done as God: He pours Himself out in selfless love. The difference is that when humans love, it hurts. We are by nature finite and limited, so that when we give, we suffer loss. Jesus shows us the mystery of God's plan for us, that when God became man, He made it possible for us to share in His divine life and love. Our nature will always be limited but, united to God in Christ, we have an infinite source of love, which we are called to tap into. In this life, we will continue to experience suffering as we love, but Christ's Resurrection proves that we are really made to live and love in heaven, where every tear will be wiped away.

The ultimate goal of salvation history is our entry into eternal life with God in heaven (cf. Catechism, no. 260).

Mother of All Virtues

Love assists us in leading virtuous lives. As Saint Thomas Aquinas writes, "Charity is the form, mover, mother, and root of all the virtues."[2] Love renders suffering bearable, and even joyful. Because I love my son or daughter, I am willing to change diapers and clean up other biological disasters. Actions which would have been repugnant without love are now embraced (or at least endured) for the sake of my beloved child. Jesus doesn't hide the fact that Christianity is difficult, but He reveals how, with love, the burdens of life become light and their yoke easy.

The theological and moral virtues empower us to overcome the world in Christ. Faith and hope allow us to see that our real home is not here, but in heaven.

> Therefore, since we are surrounded by so great a cloud of witnesses, let us also lay aside every weight, and the sin which clings so closely, and let us run with perseverance the race that is set before us, looking to Jesus the pioneer and perfecter of our faith, who for the joy that was set before him endured the cross, despising the shame, and is seated at the right hand of the throne of God (Heb. 12:1-2).

It will take prudence to find our way, and temperance to overcome the passing attractions of this world. As sons of God, we must manifest our concern for our brothers and sisters through justice, and press on with fortitude toward the upward call of God in Christ Jesus (cf. Phil. 3:14).

---

[2] Saint Thomas Aquinas, On Charity (*De Caritate*), trans. Lottie H. Kendzierski (Milwaukee, WI: Marquette University Press, 1984), p. 35, art. 3.

The life of virtue is both essential and practical. By virtue we are formed into real men through God's grace. Getting to heaven isn't easy. Without grace it is impossible. But, how we get there is simple. Jesus has given us the questions to the final exam in advance. He has told us exactly what will be required of us if we want to inherit eternal life.

> Then the King will say to those at his right hand, "Come, O blessed of my Father, inherit the kingdom prepared for you from the foundation of the world; for I was hungry and you gave me food, I was thirsty and you gave me drink, I was a stranger and you welcomed me, I was naked and you clothed me, I was sick and you visited me, I was in prison and you came to me. . . . Truly, I say to you, as you did it to one of the least of these my brethren, you did it to me" (Mt. 25:34-36, 40).

Charity begins at home. As we review the acts of love that lead to salvation, we realize that most of them can be performed daily within our families. But, there is more. We must recognize what God is doing in human history. He is taking the broken family of Adam and reconstituting it as the "Family of God" in Christ Jesus. If we are to live the virtues, we must have our Father's heart. God loves, and so must we. The test is simple. We must love God, and our neighbor for God's sake.

> If any one says, "I love God," and hates his brother, he is a liar; for he who does not love his brother whom he has seen, cannot love God whom he has not seen (1 Jn. 4:20).

A man of God must imitate the love of God and work to build up the Family of God on earth.

Questions

1. As we have read, love is the capstone of all the virtues. Read Philippians 1:9. If love is willing the good for others, why would an increase in knowledge be helpful?

_____

_____

2. According to 1 John 5:3, how can we know that we are living lives of love?

_____

_____

3. 1 Corinthians 13:4-7 gives us a means of determining whether our love is based on emotions or on an act of the will. How does our love compare with this description?

_____

_____

4. Love is a decision. Joshua, one of the great heroes of salvation history, challenged the People of God with making a decision (see Josh. 24:15). What is your decision for you and your house?

_____

_____

5. Saint Paul calls us to have the "mind of Christ" (see Memory Verse, p. 113). Read Philippians 3:4-8.

a. How does Saint Paul apply the selflessness of Christ to his own life?

_____

_____

b. How can this selflessness be made manifest in our lives?

_____

_____

Christ Gives Us the Example of Love

6. Jesus provides us with the perfect example of love. What can we learn from the following passages?

a. 1 John 3:17-18. How is love manifested?

_____

_____

b. 1 John 4:7-12. What is the source of our ability to love?

_____

_____

c. John 3:16 and Romans 5:5-8. How did God manifest His love for us?

_____

_____

d. Ephesians 5:2. What should be our goal in life?

_____

_____

Jesus Gives Us the Power to Love

7. How does Jesus make it possible for us to live godly love? (See John 14:15-17.)

_____

_____

8. According to John 15:1-5, how can we persevere in love?

_____

_____

9. Read 1 Corinthians 10:16. What incredible gift has Christ left us to remain united with Him?

_____

_____

10. According to Galatians 2:20, what is the effect of being united to Christ's body?

_____

_____

11. What is the effect of being in communion with the resurrected Christ? (See 2 Corinthians 6:16.)

_____

_____

12. Read Philippians 1:21. How can we imitate Saint Paul's unity with Christ?

_____

_____

13. In John 15:13, Jesus gives us the description of perfect love. Given what Jesus tells us about being true disciples in John 13:35, how are we to live our commitment to Christ, as it affects:

a. Our faith?

_____

_____

b. Our family?

_____

_____

c. Our culture?

_____

_____

The theological virtues are increased through action and through prayer. The following is a traditional prayer, given to us by the Church. We ought to ask God for His help whenever we need it. Can you make an effort to pray this Act of Love each day this week?

Act of Love
O my God, I love You above all things, with my whole heart and soul, because You are all-good and worthy of all my love. I love my neighbor as myself for the love of You. I forgive all who have injured me, and ask pardon of all whom I have injured. Amen.

Memory Verse
"Have this mind among yourselves,
which was in Christ Jesus,
who, though he was in the form of God,
did not count equality with God a thing to be grasped,
but emptied himself, taking the form of a servant,
being born in the likeness of men. And being found
in human form he humbled himself
and became obedient unto death,
even death on a cross."
Philippians 2:5-8

Chapter 9
Final Thoughts

Now that we have finished our examination of the virtues, it is important to remind ourselves that, although we distinguish among the various virtues, there is unity among them. For example, the virtue of love is both prudent and courageous, and the virtue of hope is temperate and faithful. Thus, the truly virtuous man excels in all the virtues.

As we stated earlier, the cardinal virtues perfect man's natural powers. If we stop there, however, we fall short of our true calling: participation in the divine life of the Trinity. The cardinal virtues prepare the way, but the theological virtues are the destination. To simply be courageous or just is not enough; we are called to live in faith, hope, and love.

Aristotle long ago observed, at the end of his treatise on virtue, that the goal of virtue is friendship. Without virtue, real friendship and happiness are not possible. The goal of the moral life is far more than avoiding serious sin or simply being a law-abiding citizen. In a real sense, the purpose of the moral life is to become the kind of person who can be a good friend. The cardinal virtues and the other natural virtues empower us to be good friends, to live in communities where friendship flourishes, and thus to fulfill Jesus' command to love our neighbor as ourselves. They enable us to act according to our proper nature, which in turn is the path to happiness.

The theological virtues take this friendship to another level. Saint Thomas Aquinas accepted Aristotle's conclusion about the virtues ending in friendship. However, Saint Thomas explained that ultimately the goal of the virtues is friendship with God. This friendship with God is impossible with the natural virtues alone, which is why we need the theological virtues. These virtues equip us to live as God's friends. Thus Saint Thomas teaches that the theological virtue of charity is nothing other than our friendship with God: "Charity is the friendship of man for God."[1] Therefore, Saint Thomas quotes Jesus: "You are my friends. . . . No longer do I call you servants" (Jn. 15:14-15).

Path to Happiness

Building our lives on the rock-solid habits of the virtues gives us the stability and strength of character that enable us to endure the storms of life. Without such a foundation it is easy to falter and fail. We are wounded and weak because of the Fall and concupiscence. In addition, we are further weakened every time we give in to our passions. We have made our passions strong through bad habit, while our will to do good is weak. This problem cannot be solved by "values" alone, but only by the firm resolve and constant effort to reform our will.

Motivated by love, we can be transformed by the noble actions that lead to good habits and end in solid character. Over time, through God's grace and our arduous effort, we can build up the habits that dispose us to be virtuous. This positive inclination, which the virtues bestow upon us, along with the grace of God, liberates our will to do the good we desire to do, rather than capitulating to our passions. This is what Saint Paul meant when he spoke of the "glorious liberty of the children of God" (Rom. 8:21). In the end, the moral life is about liberty or slavery: the liberty that comes only through virtuous living (acting according to a properly ordered nature), or the slavery that comes from surrendering to our passions and desires (acting according to a disordered nature).

---

[1] *Summa*, IIa IIae, q. 23, art. 1.

The Challenge to Run the Race

Our culture is suffering from a lack of virtue. Each one of us has the responsibility to bring virtue, and not simply values, back to society. This is accomplished by *being* virtuous and instilling good habits in our families. By practicing the virtues, we bear witness to others of a more rewarding way of life.

God has provided us with all the means for becoming truly virtuous men. We have the Church, which feeds and strengthens us through the Scriptures and the sacraments. We also have the living presence of the Holy Spirit within us (cf. Acts 2:38-42). We are like athletes in training, and we need to use the tools at our disposal to equip ourselves for the life we are called to live.

A life of virtue may be very difficult at times, but it is possible. The saints demonstrate the fact that virtue can be lived and, at times, heroically. Reading the lives of the saints is an effective way to keep our own lives inspired by the virtues. Imitation is one of the most effective methods of learning, and the saints offer compelling examples for today's men to imitate.

The means are at your disposal. The invitation is yours. Will you become a man of God? History repeatedly shows us that other men have taken the challenge and, in Christ, they have overcome the world by overcoming their own wounded nature. The world is in desperate need of men like this today—men of whom the world is not worthy (cf. Heb 11:36-38). They are waiting for you. What are you waiting for?

Questions

We have now reached the end of our study on the virtues. Read Hebrews 11. This passage is filled with examples of great men of God—men *of whom the world was not worthy* (Heb. 11:38).

1. Hebrews 11 tells us about some of the great men of faith in the Old Testament. What does heroic faith require from a godly man today?

_____

_____

2. Taking a look at some of the main characters of salvation history, what do you think separated them from ordinary men? And what do you think some of their greatest challenges were in remaining faithful?

a. Noah (Gen. 6-9)

_____

_____

b. Abraham (Gen. 12-22)

_____

_____

c. Moses (Ex. 2-24, 32-33)

_____

_____

3. Read Romans 15:1-7 and 1 Corinthians 10:1-13. Why is a knowledge of biblical salvation history so important if we want to be men of God?

_____

_____

4. Now is the time to make decisions. Briefly review the seven virtues we have covered: wisdom, justice, fortitude, temperance, faith, hope, and charity. How does your new perspective change the way you want to approach life?

_____

_____

_____

_____

5. Specifically, which virtue(s) are you going to work on?

_____

_____

_____

6. What specific actions can you begin to take today to grow in this virtue?

_____

_____

_____

_____

7. How can you improve your prayer life to be better connected with Christ?

_____

_____

_____

Plan of Action Grid
Specific Actions to Grow in Virtue

Virtue	Short-term	Long-term
Prudence		
Justice		
Fortitude		
Temperance		
Faith		
Hope		
Charity		

An athlete wouldn't dream of training without consistent meals and exercise. The pursuit of virtue is similar. We must draw our nourishment from God, through prayer and the grace which comes through the sacraments. And we must choose to do the right thing consistently.

Prayer Before Work
Direct, we beg You, O Lord, our actions by Your holy inspirations, and grant that we may carry them out with Your gracious assistance, that every prayer and work of ours may begin always with You, and through You be happily ended. Amen.

Memory Verse
"I can do all things in him who strengthens me."
Philippians 4:13

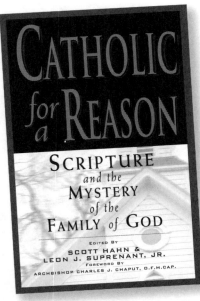

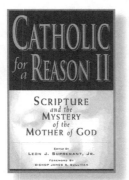